Developmental Mathematics

Solution Manual

LEVEL TWELVE

THOUSANDS AND LARGE NUMBERS

CONCEPTS & SKILLS

12

L. George Saad, Ph. D.
Professor Emeritus
Long Island University

1   THOUSANDS

10 hundreds make 1 thousand

a.

1 thousand
We write: 1,000

b.

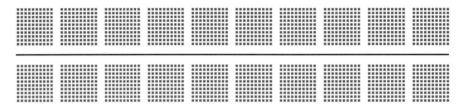

2 thousands
We write: 2,000

c.

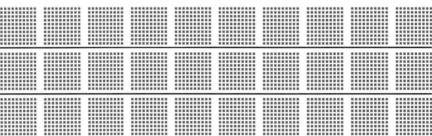

3 thousands
We write: _____3,000_____

How much money is each amount?

a.	10 one-hundred dollar bills?	$1,000
b.	30 one-hundred dollar bills?	$3,000
c.	80 one-hundred dollar bills?	$8,000
d.	100 one-hundred dollar bills?	$10,000
e.	400 one-hundred dollar bills?	$40,000
f.	100 ten-dollar bills?	$1,000
g.	700 ten-dollar bills?	$7,000
h.	800 ten-dollar bills?	$8,000

APPLICATIONS

What is the number?

1. You have 8 boxes, with 1000 stamps in each box.
   How many stamps do you have? _____ 8,000

2. A farmer has 19 piles, with 1,000 oranges in each pile.
   How many oranges does he have? _____ 19,000

3. A theatre which has 1,000 seats
   was full for a whole week.
   How many persons attended? _____ 7,000

4. 25 students won scholarships of $1,000 each.
   How much was the total amount? _____ $25,000

5. John's monthly take-home pay check is $1,000.
   How much does he receive in a year? _____ $12,000

6. A restaurant serves 1,000 customers every day.
   How many customers are served during July? _____ 31,000

7. On the average, every day 1,000 cars go through a toll booth.
   In all, how many cars go through the booth in a year? _____ 365,000

8. On the average, 1,000 persons use a library every week.
   In all, how many persons use the library in a year?
   (The year is 52 weeks). _____ 52,000

9. A bank teller has 17 packages of money bills:
   $1,000 each
   How much money does she have? _____ $17,000

10. An oil company has 28 trucks with 1000-gallon tanks.
    In all, how much oil can these trucks carry? _____ 28,000 gallons

Write the number:

a. What number is the same as 10 hundreds? _____ 1,000
b. What number is the same as 60 hundreds? _____ 6,000
c. What number is the same as 80 hundreds? _____ 8,000
d. What number is the same as 100 hundreds? _____ 10,000
e. What number is the same as 400 hundreds? _____ 40,000
f. What number is the same as 900 hundreds? _____ 90,000

Date _____

LARGE MONEY BILLS

- Do you know that there is a $1,000 bill? Printed on it is the portrait of Grover Cleveland, who was elected twice to the presidency: 1885-1889 and 1893-1897.

- Also, there is a $10,000 bill. Printed on it is the portrait of Salmon Chase, who was Secretary of the Treasury in President Abraham Lincoln's cabinet.

- Also, there is a $100,000 bill. Printed on it is the portrait of Woodrow Wilson, who was the president of the United States of America for two terms: 1913-1917 and 1917-1921.

APPLICATIONS

How much money is pictured in the box?

a.  ___$3,000___	b.  ___$30,000___	c.  ___$300,000___
d.  ___$4,000___	e.  ___$40,000___	f. 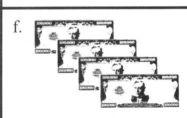 ___$400,000___

APPLICATIONS

How much money is pictured below?

a.

$241,000

b.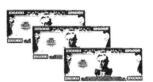

$320,000

c.

$103,000

How much money is each amount?

a. 9 one-hundred-thousand dollar bills. $900,000

b. 15 one-thousand dollar bills. $15,000

c. 6 ten-thousand dollar bills, and
4 one-thousand dollar bills. $64,000

d. 3 one-hundred-thousand dollar bills,
6 ten thousand-dollar bills, and
5 one-thousand-dollar bills. $365,000

e. 8 one-hundred-thousand dollar bills,
and 7 one-thousand dollar bills. $807,000

f. 9 one-hundred-thousand-dollar bills,
and 4 ten-thousand dollar bills. $940,000

g. 10 ten-thousand dollar bills. $100,000

h. 60 ten-thousand dollar bills $600,000

2 ADDING

Example 1.

a. Tom has $5,000.
   Dan has $3,000 more than Tom.
   - How much does Dan have? <u>$8,000</u>
   - How much do they have altogether? <u>$13,000</u>

b. In a village there are 4,000 men,
   3,000 women, and 2,000 children.
   How many persons live in this village? <u>9,000</u>

c. In a school district, there are 4,000 students
   in the elementary schools, 2,000 in
   the junior high school, and 2,000 students
   in the high school.
   How many students are in the district? <u>8,000</u>

d. In a college, there are 5,000 women.
   There are 2,000 more men than women.
   - How many men are there? <u>7,000</u>
   - How many students are in the college? <u>12,000</u>

EXERCISES

Write the answer:

a.	4,000 + 3,000 =	7,000	b.	2,000 + 7,000 =	9,000
c.	1,000 + 4,000 =	5,000	d.	5,000 + 1,000 =	6,000
e.	4,000 + 5,000 =	9,000	f.	3,000 + 2,000 =	5,000
g.	2,000 + 8,000 =	10,000	h.	9,000 + 1,000 =	10,000
i.	4,000 + 6,000 =	10,000	j.	5,000 + 5,000 =	10,000
k.	6,000 + 5,000 =	11,000	l.	9,000 + 9,000 =	18,000
m.	4,000 + 9,000 =	13,000	n.	8,000 + 7,000 =	15,000
o.	30,000 + 40,000 =	70,000	p.	50,000 + 40,000 =	90,000
q.	20,000 + 40,000 =	60,000	r.	80,000 + 20,000 =	100,000
s.	500,000 + 200,000 =	700,000	t.	300,000 + 300,000 =	600,000
u.	300,000 + 100,000 =	400,000	v.	100,000 + 600,000 =	700,000

EXERCISES

Add:

a.   70,000 + 8,000   =   _78,000_   b.   30,000 + 9,000   =   _39,000_
c.   21,000 + 5,000   =   _26,000_   d.   31,000 + 4,000   =   _35,000_
e.   25,000 + 5,000   =   _30,000_   f.   14,000 + 6,000   =   _20,000_
g.   43,000 + 8,000   =   _51,000_   h.   35,000 + 9,000   =   _44,000_
i.   27,000 + 5,000   =   _32,000_   j.   56,000 + 6,000   =   _62,000_
k.   31,000 + 64,000 =   _95,000_   l.   48,000 + 30,000 =   _78,000_
m. 15,000 + 32,000 =   _47,000_   n.   30,000 + 25,000 =   _55,000_
o.   500,000 + 40,000 = _540,000_   p.   700,000 + 30,000 = _730,000_
q.   800,000 + 20,000 = _820,000_   r.   400,000 + 40,000 = _440,000_
s.   400,000 + 7,000 =   _407,000_   t.   900,000 + 9,000 =   _909,000_
u.   200,000 + 1,000 =   _201,000_   v.   700,000 + 3,000 =   _703,000_
w.   700,000 + 20,000 + 5,000 = _725,000_
x.   200,000 + 30,000 + 6,000 = _236,000_
y.   800,000 + 10,000 + 4,000 = _814,000_
z.   100,000 + 60,000 + 6,000 = _166,000_

APPLICATIONS

1.   A family bought a house. They paid
     $10,000 and the bank paid $50,000.
     How much did the house cost? $10,000 + $50,000 = $60,000

2.   The population of 3 villages is 9,000,
     3,000, and 6,000. How many persons
     live in the 3 villages altogether?   9,000 + 3,000 + 6,000 = 18,000

3.   A family bought a house for $85,000.
     They sold the house with a profit of $7,000.
     For how much did they sell the house? $85,000 + $ 7,000 = $92,000

4.   On Monday, a store sold goods for $15,000.
     The sales rose $3,000 daily for the next three days.
     How much were the sales on Wednesday? $15,000 + $3,000 + $3,000 = $21,000

5.   There were 92,000 books in the library.
     8,000 new books were added.
     How many books are in the library now?   92,000 + 8,000 = 100,000

Example 2.

You want to add: 231,000 + 142,000 + 24,000

Discussion:

You may use boxes as shown to the right.

- Add the ones of thousands: 7 Th's
- Add the tens of thousands: 9 tens of Th's
- Add the hundreds of thousands: 3 hundreds of Th's

THOUSANDS		
100'S	10'S	1'S
2	3	1
1	4	2
	2	4
+ 3	9	7

Example 3.

You want to add: 236,000 + 158,000 + 67,000

Discussion:

You may use boxes as shown to the right.

- Add the ones of thousands: 21 Th's
  21 Th's = 2 tens of Th's + 1 Th's
  Write 1 in the ones of Th's box, and
  remember that you have 2 tens of Th's
  to add to the tens of thousands.
- Add the tens of thousands: 16 tens of Th's
  16 tens of Th's = 1 hundred of Th's + 6 tens of Th's
  Write 6 in the tens of Th's box. Remember that you
  have 1 hundred of Th's to add to the hundreds of Th's.
- Add the hundreds of thousands: 4 hundreds of Th's
  Write 4 in the hundreds of thousands box.

THOUSANDS		
100'S	10'S	1'S
2	3	6
1	5	8
	6	7
+ 4	6	1

You may, of course, do without the boxes.

Do the following additions:

a.	b.	c.	d.
232,000	50,000	291,000	383,000
41,000	312,000	38,000	139,000
+ 106,000	+ 127,000	+ 253,000	+ 49,000
379,000	489,000	582,000	571,000

e.	f.	g.	h.
139,000	375,000	789,000	197,000
378,000	276,000	81,000	81,000
+ 94,000	+ 24,000	+ 40,000	+ 342,000
611,000	675,000	910,000	620,000

i.	j.	k.	l.
48,000	19,000	39,000	282,000
118,000	147,000	251,000	74,000
+ 35,000	+ 238,000	+ 310,000	+ 144,000
201,000	404,000	600,000	500,000

1. Last year the profits of a company were $293,000.
This year the profits have increased by $89,000.
How much are the profits this year? $382,000

2. The population of a city is 190,000 people.
With an increase of 26,000 per year, what
will the population be after two years?   242,000

3. A company owns three canning machines. The daily
production of the machines is 39,000 cans,
42,000 cans, and 28,000 cans. What is the daily
production of the three machines altogether?   109,000 cans

4. A textile firm produced three kinds of fabric:
      1st kind: 39,000 yards
      2nd kind: 84,000 yards
      3rd kind: 77,000 yards
How many yards did the company
produce of the three kinds?   200,000

5. A publishing company published a certain book
three times:
      1st time: 75,000 copies
      2nd time: 87,000 copies
      3rd time: 115,000 copies
How many copies of this book were published?   277,000

6. A, B, and C are three numbers.
A is 36,000, B is 19,000 more than A,
and C is 28,000 more than B.
What number is B? $B = 36{,}000 + 19{,}000 = 55{,}000$
What number is C? $C = 55{,}000 + 28{,}000 = 83{,}000$

7. $M = 39{,}000$
$N = M + 81{,}000$
$X = N + 25{,}000$
What number is N? $N = 39{,}000 + 81{,}000 = 120{,}000$
What number is X? $X = 120{,}000 + 25{,}000 = 145{,}000$

3 SUBTRACTING

Example 1.
   Last year, Ted's income was $9,000. He spent $7,000.
   How much did he save?

Solution:
   9 Th's - 7 Th's = 2 Th's
   So, 9,000 - 7,000 = 2,000   Ted saved $2,000.

$$\begin{array}{r} 9,000 \\ -\ 7,000 \\ \hline 2,000 \end{array}$$

Example 2.
   The population of a village is 14,000. 8,000 are males.
   How many females live in the village?

Solution:
   The number of females = 14,000 - 8,000 = 6,000

$$\begin{array}{r} 14,000 \\ -\ 8,000 \\ \hline 6,000 \end{array}$$

Example 3.
   During January 1999, a bus line carries 700,000 passengers.
   During February 1999, the number of passengers decreased by 200,000.
   How many passengers used the bus line during February 1999?

Solution:
   700, 000 - 200,000 = 500,000
   During February 1984, 500,000 passengers used the bus line.

EXERCISES

Write the answer:

1.	a. 9,000 - 4,000 =	5,000	b.	8,000 - 2,000 =	6,000
	c. 7,000 - 3,000 =	4,000	d.	6,000 - 6,000 =	0

2.	a. 11,000 - 2,000 =	9,000	b.	14,000 - 5,000 =	9,000
	c. 12,000 - 7,000 =	5,000	d.	17,000 - 9,000 =	8,000
	e. 10,000 - 4,000 =	6,000	f.	10,000 - 1,000 =	9,000

3.	a. 90,000 - 70,000 =	20,000	b.	40,000 - 30,000 =	10,000
	c. 60,000 - 40,000 =	20,000	d.	80,000 - 80,000 =	0

4.	a. 37,000 - 5,000 =	32,000	b.	86,000 - 6,000 =	80,000
	c. 950,000 - 30,000 =	920,000	d.	840,000 - 40,000 =	800,000

5.	a. 40,000 - 7,000 =	33,000	b.	90,000 - 6,000 =	84,000
	c. 31,000 - 4,000 =	27,000	d.	56,000 - 9,000 =	47,000

Example 4.
You want to subtract: 978,000 - 246,000
Discussion:
You may use boxes.

THOUSANDS		
100'S	10'S	1'S
9	7	8
2	4	6
7	3	2

(with a − sign before the second row)

- 8 Th's - 6 Th's = 2 Th's
- 7 tens of Th's - 4 tens of Th's = 3 tens of Th's
- 9 hundreds of Th's - 2 hundreds of TH's = __7 hundreds of Th's__
The answer is __732,000__

Example 5.
Do the subtraction to the right.

THOUSANDS		
100'S	10'S	1'S
6	5	1
2	8	7
3	6	4

(with a − sign before the second row)

Solution:
- 11 Th's - 7 Th's = 4 Th's
- 14 tens of Th's - 8 tens of Th's = 6 tens of Th's
- 5 hundreds of Th's - 2 hundreds of Th's = __3 hundreds of Th's__
The answer is __364,000__

Example 6.
Do the subtraction to the right.

THOUSANDS		
100'S	10'S	1'S
7	2	3
1	9	8
5	2	5

(with a − sign before the second row)

Solution:
- 13 Th's - 8 Th's = 5 Th
- 11 tens of Th's - 9 tens of Th's = 2 tens of Th's
- 6 hundreds of Th's - 1 hundred of Th's = __5 hundreds of Th's__
The answer is __525,000__

You may, of course, do without the boxes.
Do the following subtractions:

a.	b.	c.	d.
642,000 - 118,000 **524,000**	913,000 - 851,000 62,000	835,000 - 149,000 686,000	740,000 - 395,000 345,000
e.	**f.**	**g.**	**h.**
810,000 - 283,000 527,000	805,000 - 463,000 342,000	901,000 - 265,000 636,000	800,000 - 365,000 435,000
i.	**j.**	**k.**	**l.**
834,000 - 96,000 738,000	470,000 - 84,000 386,000	700,000 - 98,000 602,000	107,000 - 88,000 19,000

Date _____

EXERCISES

Subtract:

1. a. $9,000 - 4,000 = \underline{5,000}$ b. $14,000 - 5,000 = \underline{9,000}$

    c. $8,000 - 1,000 = \underline{7,000}$ d. $12,000 - 7,000 = \underline{5,000}$

    e. $90,000 - 80,000 = \underline{10,000}$ f. $800,000 - 300,000 = \underline{500,000}$

    g. $40,000 - 30,000 = \underline{10,000}$ h. $900,000 - 500,000 = \underline{400,000}$

    i. $25,000 - 5,000 = \underline{20,000}$ j. $85,000 - 3,000 = \underline{82,000}$

    k. $48,000 - 8,000 = \underline{40,000}$ l. $46,000 - 5,000 = \underline{41,000}$

    m. $930,000 - 30,000 = \underline{900,000}$ n. $740,000 - 30,000 = \underline{710,000}$

    o. $750,000 - 50,000 = \underline{700,000}$ p. $680,000 - 50,000 = \underline{630,000}$

    q. $49,000 - 23,000 = \underline{26,000}$ r. $78,000 - 28,000 = \underline{50,000}$

    s. $85,000 - 31,000 = \underline{54,000}$ t. $69,000 - 39,000 = \underline{30,000}$

2.

a.	b.	c.	d.
798,000 - 261,000 537,000	685,000 - 243,000 442,000	291,000 - 38,000 253,000	465,000 - 217,000 248,000
e.	f.	g.	h.
715,000 - 496,000 219,000	823,000 - 165,000 658,000	760,000 - 194,000 566,000	640,000 - 295,000 345,000
i.	j.	k.	l.
610,000 - 441,000 169,000	910,000 - 284,000 626,000	703,000 - 151,000 552,000	302,000 - 92,000 210,000
m.	n.	o.	p.
801,000 - 148,000 653,000	603,000 - 298,000 305,000	700,000 - 125,000 575,000	800,000 - 194,000 606,000

APPLICATIONS

1. Carol is a real estate saleswoman.
   She sold two houses for $150,000.
   One of the house was sold for $60,000.
   How much was the price of the second house? $150,000 - $60,000 = $90,000

2. The number of books in a library
   increased from 197,000 to 203,000.
   How many books were added?   203,000 - 197,000 = 6,000

3. The population of a village is 14,000.
   5,000 are men and 6,000 are women.
   How many children are there?
   a. 5,000 + 6,000 = 11,000
   b. 14,000 - 11,000 = 3,000

4. Every year John gets an increase of $3,000.
   This year his salary is $25,000.
   a. What was his salary last year?
   b. What will his salary be next year?
   a. $25,000 - $3,000 = $22,000
   b. $25,000 + $3,000 = $28,000

5. In three years the profits of a company
   totaled $915,000. The profits in the first
   year were $276,000 and in the second
   year were $385,000.
   What were the profits in the third year?
   a. $276,000 + $385,000 = $661,000
   b. $915,000 - $661,000 = $254,000

6. You started with a number, added 30,000,
   and then subtracted 90,000.
   The answer was 10,000.
   What was the number?
   a. 10,000 + 90,000 = 100,000
   b. 100,000 - 30,000 = 70,000

7. A, B, and C are three numbers.
   A is 192,000, B is 89,000 more than A,
   and C is 65,000 less than B.
   What number is C?
   a. B = 192,000 + 89,000 = 281,000
   b. C = 281,000 - 65,000 = 216,000

8. You subtracted a number from 795,000
   and added 134,000.
   The answer was 600,000.
   What was the number?
   a. 600,000 - 134,000 = 466,000
   b. 795,000 - 466,000 = 329,000

9. The difference between two numbers is 20,000.
   The smaller number is 170,000.
   Find the other number.   170,000 + 20,000 = 190,000

Example 1:

There are 1,000 stamps in each envelope.
In all, how many stamps are there?

Discussion:

- There are 3 rows of envelopes.
- In each row, there are 4 envelopes.
- In all, there are 3 x 4 = 12 envelopes.
- In all, there are 3 x 4,000 = 12,000 stamps.

Similarly:

a. 8 x 7,000 = __56,000__	b. 9 x 6,000 = __54,000__
c. 2 x 5,000 = __10,000__	d. 5 x 8,000 = __40,000__
e. 9 x 9,000 = __81,000__	f. 4 x 5,000 = __20,000__
g. 7 x 6,000 = __42,000__	h. 5 x 6,000 = __30,000__

Example 2:

Suppose you have 7 very long strings of beads with 3,000 in each string.
A part of the arrangement is shown below.
In all, how many beads are there?

- You may see the beads as 7 sets with 3,000 beads in each set.
  In all, there are 7 x 3,000 = 21,000 beads.
- You also may see the beads as 3,000 sets with 7 beads in each set.
  In all, there are 3,000 x 7 = 21,000 beads.

Similarly:

a. 3 x 9,000 = __27,000__ 9,000 x 3 = __27,000__	b. 4 x 6,000 = __24,000__ 6,000 x 4 = __24,000__
c. 6 x 8,000 = __48,000__ 8,000 x 6 = __48,000__	d. 7,000 x 3 = __21,000__ 3 x 7,000 = __21,000__
e. 5 x 8,000 = __40,000__ 8,000 x 5 = __40,000__	f. 8,000 x 8 = __64,000__ 8 x 8,000 = __64,000__

EXERCISES

Write the answer:

1. a. 3 x 6,000 =   18,000   b. 7 x 4,000 =   28,000
    c. 6 x 2,000 =   12,000   d. 6 x 5,000 =   30,000
    e. 9 x 8,000 =   72,000   f. 6 x 7,000 =   42,000

2. a. 4,000 x 5 =   20,000   b. 5,000 x 4 =   20,000
    c. 7,000 x 8 =   56,000   d. 9,000 x 6 =   54,000
    e. 6,000 x 7 =   42,000   f. 8,000 x 5 =   40,000

3. a. 5 x 102,000 =   510,000   b. 3 x 294,000 =   882,000
    c. 9 x 104,000 =   936,000   d. 4 x 208,000 =   832,000
    e. 4 x 236,000 =   944,000   f. 8 x 89,000 =   712,000

4. a. 324,000 x 3 =   972,000   b. 164,000 x 5 =   820,000
    c. 125,000 x 6 =   750,000   d. 208,000 x 4 =   832,000
    e. 79,000 x 9 =   711,000   f. 85,000 x 8 =   680,000

APPLICATIONS

1. A canning plant produces 185,000 cans a day.
    How many cans are produced in the 5
    working days of the week?   5 x 185,000 = 925,000

2. A textile factory produced 74,000 yards of
    material. They were sold for $3 a yard.
    For how much were they sold?   74,000 x $3 = $222,000

3. A jet airliner covered six 5,000-mile trips and   a. 6 x 5,000 = 30,000
    eight 4,000-mile trips.   b. 8 x 4,000 = 32,000
    Altogether, how many miles did the jet cover?   c. Altogether: 62,000

4. M = 4,000
    N = twice M
    P = 9 times N.   N = 2 x 4,000 = 8,000
    What number is P?   P = 9 x 8,000 = 72,000

5. A is 85,000, B is 79,000 more
    than A, and C is 3 times B.   B = 164,000
    What number is C?   C = 3 x 164,000 = 492,000

15

A

Example 3.

A garment factory produces 23,000 suits each month.
How many suits are produced in a year?

```
  23
x 12
  46
  23
 276
```

Discussion:
- The situation calls for the multiplication: 12 x 23,000.
- The answer to (12 x 23,000) is the same as
  (12 x 23) in thousands.
  12 x 23 = 276
  12 x 23,000 = 276,000

Example 4.

Find the answer: 29 x 32,000

```
  29
x 32
  58
  87
 928
```

a. 29 x 32 = __928__
b. 29 x 32,000 = __928,000__

Example 5.

Find the answer: 25,000 x 38

```
  25
x 38
 200
  75
 950
```

a. 25 x 38 = __950__
b. 25,000 x 38 = __950,000__

EXERCISES

Multiply:

a. 23 x 25,000	b. 35 x 12,000	c. 43,000 x 18
__575,000__	__420,000__	__774,000__
d. 26,000 x 32	e. 17,000 x 29	f. 36 x 25,000
__832,000__	__493,000__	__900,000__

APPLICATIONS

1. One week, a poultry farm produced
    18,000 dozens of eggs.
    How many eggs were produced that week? $\underline{18,000 \times 12 = 216,000}$

2. The monthly expenses of a company
    is $38,000.
    How much are the yearly expenses? $\underline{12 \times \$38,000 = \$456,000}$

3. The textile factory produces 14,000
    yards of curtain material each week.
    How many yards of material are produced
    in one year? $\underline{52 \times 14,000 = 728,000}$

4. A builder built 25 houses, with
    the cost of $39,000 per house.
    How much did the project cost? $\underline{25 \times \$39,000 = 975,000}$

5. Find the answer:
    a. (24 x 32,000) - 76,000   b. (41,000 x 16) + 25,000

    $\underline{768,000 - 76,000 = 692,000}$ $\underline{656,000 + 25,000 = 681,000}$

6. Find the sum of (28 x 24,000)
        and   (17,000 x 15)

    $\underline{672,000 + 255,000 = 927,000}$

7. Find the difference between
    (16,000 x 28) and (39,000 x 14)

    $\underline{546,000 - 448,000 = 98,000}$

Level 12

5   DIVIDING

Example 1.

You have 2,000 items. Below is a picture of a part of the arrangement.

Discussion:

    a. You may see the arrangement as 2 equivalent sets.
The following equation applies: $2,000 \div 2 = 1,000$
Result: 1,000 items in each set.

    b. You also may see the arrangement as 2 equivalent sets.
The following equation applies: $2,000 \div 2 = 1,000$
Result: 1,000 sets are made.

Note:

In both cases, the equation "$2,000 \div 2 = 1,000$" applies, but in a, the answer is "1,000 items in each set", and, in b, the answer is "1,000 sets are made".

Example 2.

You have 8,000 stamps. Below is a picture of a part of the arrangement.

Discussion:

    a. Divide them equally into 4 sets.
- You have 8 identical rows.
- You divide them equally into 4 sets.

      $8 \div 4 = 2$ 2 rows in each set
      $8,000 \div 4 = 2,000$ 2,000 stamps in each set.

    b. Make them into sets with 4 stamps in each set.
- Looking vertically, you see that there are 1,000 groups, 8 stamps each.
- Each of these groups may be made into 2 fours.
1,000 groups make 2,000 fours.
- $8,000 \div 4 = 2,000$ 2,000 sets are made.

Note:

In both cases, the equation "$8,000 \div 4 = 2,000$" applies, but in example a, the answer is "2,000 items in each set" and, in example b, the answer is "2,000 sets are made."

APPLICATIONS

What does the answer tell?

1. a. A stationery store received 24,000 pens in 4 boxes, with the same number of pens in each box.

$24,000 \div 4 = 6,000$ <u>6,000 pens in each box</u>

    b. A stationery store received 24,000 pens in packs, 4 pens each.

$24,000 \div 4 = 6,000$ <u>6,000 packs were received</u>

2. a. A bank teller has $40,000 in five-dollar bills.

$\$40,000 \div \$5 = 8,000$ <u>8,000 bills</u>

    b. A bank teller has $40,000 in 5 packs, with the same amount in each pack.

$\$40,000 \div 5 = \$8,000$ <u>$8,000 in each pack</u>

3. An auto factory charged a dealer $21,000 for 3 identical cars.

$\$21,000 \div 3 = \$7,000$ <u>$7,000 paid for each car</u>

4. A supermarket collected $60,000 selling cookies at $2 a pound.

$\$60,000 \div \$2 = 30,000$ <u>30,000 pounds were sold</u>

5. A soda factory produced 400,000 cans in 8-can packs.

$400,000 \div 8 = 50,000$ <u>50,000 packs were produced</u>

EXERCISES

Write the answer:

$42,000 \div 7 = $ <u>6,000</u>	$24,000 \div 4 = $ <u>6,000</u>	$12,000 \div 6 = $ <u>2,000</u>
$35,000 \div 5 = $ <u>7,000</u>	$12,000 \div 3 = $ <u>4,000</u>	$14,000 \div 7 = $ <u>2,000</u>
$32,000 \div 8 = $ <u>4,000</u>	$18,000 \div 6 = $ <u>3,000</u>	$8,000 \div 2 = $ <u>4,000</u>
$6,000 \div 6 = $ <u>1,000</u>	$54,000 \div 9 = $ <u>6,000</u>	$24,000 \div 8 = $ <u>3,000</u>
$16,000 \div 2 = $ <u>8,000</u>	$21,000 \div 7 = $ <u>3,000</u>	$4,000 \div 4 = $ <u>1,000</u>
$8,000 \div 8 = $ <u>1,000</u>	$25,000 \div 5 = $ <u>5,000</u>	$28,000 \div 7 = $ <u>4,000</u>
$18,000 \div 9 = $ <u>2,000</u>	$36,000 \div 4 = $ <u>9,000</u>	$16,000 \div 8 = $ <u>2,000</u>
$10,000 \div 5 = $ <u>2,000</u>	$14,000 \div 2 = $ <u>7,000</u>	$27,000 \div 3 = $ <u>9,000</u>
$49,000 \div 7 = $ <u>7,000</u>	$15,000 \div 3 = $ <u>5,000</u>	$54,000 \div 6 = $ <u>9,000</u>

A

Example 3.

Do the division to the right.

Dicussion:

The number is made of

4 hundreds of thousands,

6 tens of thousands, and

8 thousands.

You divide in three steps:

- 4H's of Th's ÷ 2 = 2H's of Th's
- 6T's of Th's ÷ 2 = 3T's of Th's
- 8 Th's ÷ 2 = 4Th's

The answer is 234 Th's which is written ___234,000___

$$\frac{234{,}000}{2)\overline{468{,}000}}$$

Example 4.

Do the division to the right.

Discussion:

The dividend is composed of: 3H's of Th's,

9T's of Th's, and 5 Th's

You divide step by step.

- 3H's of Th's ÷ 5 = 0H's of Th's and 3H's of Th's remain.
- 39 T's of Th's ÷ 5 = 7T's of Th's and 4 T's of Th's remain.
- 45 Th's ÷ 5 = 9Th's.

The answer is 079 Th's which is written ___79,000___

$$\frac{079{,}000}{5)\overline{395{,}000}}$$

Example 5.

You multiplied a number by 25.

The answer was 675,000.

What was the number?

Discussion:

- The situation calls for the division: 675,000 ÷ 25.
- 675,000 is the same as 675 thousands.
  675 Th's ÷ 25 = 27 Th's
- So, 675,000 ÷ 25 = 27,000

```
    027          027,000
25)675       25)675,000
   50            50
  175           175
  175           175
```

Example 6.

Do the division:

```
     015,000
38)570,000
   38
   190
   190
```

Example 7.

Do the division:

```
      006,000
125)750,000
    750
```

EXERCISES

1.

a. $\dfrac{111,000}{5)555,000}$	b. $\dfrac{210,000}{3)630,000}$	c. $\dfrac{211,000}{4)844,000}$	d. $\dfrac{342,000}{2)684,000}$
e. $\dfrac{320,000}{3)960,000}$	f. $\dfrac{120,000}{4)480,000}$	g. $\dfrac{401,000}{2)802,000}$	h. $\dfrac{102,000}{3)306,000}$
i. $\dfrac{181,000}{4)724,000}$	j. $\dfrac{131,000}{5)655,000}$	k. $\dfrac{141,000}{7)987,000}$	l. $\dfrac{081,000}{8)648,000}$
m. $\dfrac{219,000}{4)876,000}$	n. $\dfrac{319,000}{3)957,000}$	o. $\dfrac{349,000}{2)698,000}$	p. $\dfrac{112,000}{8)896,000}$
q. $\dfrac{144,000}{3)432,000}$	r. $\dfrac{234,000}{4)936,000}$	s. $\dfrac{079,000}{5)395,000}$	t. $\dfrac{125,000}{7)875,000}$
u. $\dfrac{407,000}{2)814,000}$	v. $\dfrac{305,000}{3)915,000}$	w. $\dfrac{206,000}{4)824,000}$	x. $\dfrac{103,000}{7)721,000}$

2.

a.
$$
\begin{array}{r}
019,000 \\
\hline
15)285,000 \\
15 \\
\hline
135 \\
135 \\
\hline
\end{array}
$$

b.
$$
\begin{array}{r}
031,000 \\
\hline
25)775,000 \\
75 \\
\hline
25 \\
25 \\
\hline
\end{array}
$$

c.
$$
\begin{array}{r}
036,000 \\
\hline
18)648,000 \\
54 \\
\hline
108 \\
108 \\
\hline
\end{array}
$$

d.
$$
\begin{array}{r}
034,000 \\
\hline
24)816,000 \\
72 \\
\hline
96 \\
96 \\
\hline
\end{array}
$$

e.
$$
\begin{array}{r}
025,000 \\
\hline
34)850,000 \\
68 \\
\hline
170 \\
170 \\
\hline
\end{array}
$$

f.
$$
\begin{array}{r}
030,000 \\
\hline
24)720,000 \\
72 \\
\hline
\end{array}
$$

g.
$$
\begin{array}{r}
024,000 \\
\hline
35)840,000 \\
70 \\
\hline
140 \\
140 \\
\hline
\end{array}
$$

h.
$$
\begin{array}{r}
015,000 \\
\hline
46)690,000 \\
46 \\
\hline
230 \\
230 \\
\hline
\end{array}
$$

i.
$$
\begin{array}{r}
028,000 \\
\hline
25)700,000 \\
50 \\
\hline
200 \\
200 \\
\hline
\end{array}
$$

j.
$$
\begin{array}{r}
025,000 \\
\hline
32)800,000 \\
64 \\
\hline
160 \\
160 \\
\hline
\end{array}
$$

k.
$$
\begin{array}{r}
025,000 \\
\hline
24)600,000 \\
48 \\
\hline
120 \\
120 \\
\hline
\end{array}
$$

l.
$$
\begin{array}{r}
004,000 \\
\hline
125)500,000 \\
500 \\
\hline
\end{array}
$$

APPLICATIONS

1. A stationery store received two shipments of
   pens: 9 boxes with 3,000 pens in each box,
   and 5,000 packs with 3 pens in each pack.
   In all, how many pens were received?

   a. $9 \times 3,000 = 27,000$
   b. $5,000 \times 3 = 15,000$
   c. In all: 42,000

2. Sue, a bank teller, has 2,000 five-dollar
   bills and 1,000 ten dollar bills.
   How much money does she have?

   a. $2,000 \times \$5 = \$10,000$
   b. $1,000 \times \$10 = \$10,000$
   c. In all: $20,000

3. A department store received 2,000
   boxes with 3 shirts in each box.
   All shirts were sold for $5 each.
   How much money was the total sale?

   a. $2,000 \times 3 = 6,000$
   b. $6,000 \times \$5 = \$30,000$

4. During the last six months, a jet liner covered
   186,000 miles. Assuming that it flies the same
   trips each month,
   a. How many miles does it cover each month?
   b. How many miles does it cover in 5 months?

   $186,000 \div 6 = 031,000$
   $5 \times 31,000 = 155,000$

5. In the supply room there are 12,000 pencils
   in 6-pencil packs, and 12,000 erasers in
   4-eraser packs.
   How many packs are there?

   a. $12,000 \div 6 = 2,000$
   b. $12,000 \div 4 = 3,000$
   c. In all: 5,000

6. A bank teller has $31,000.
   She has 10 one-hundred-dollar bills, and
   the rest in five-dollar bills.
   How many five-dollar bills does she have?

   a. $10 \times \$100 = \$1,000$
   b. $\$31,000 - \$1,000 = \$30,000$
   c. $\$30,000 \div 5 = \$6,000$

7. Find the number which is 39,000 less than 8 times 63,000.

a. $8 \times 63,000 = 504,000$

b. $504,000 - 39,000 = 465,000$

8. Find the number which is 4 times the sum of 29,000 and 148,000.

a. $29,000 + 148,000 = 177,000$

b. $4 \times 177,000 = 708,000$

9. You multiplied a number by 8 and then added 18,000. The answer was 418,000.
   What was the number?

a. $418,000 - 18,000 = 400,000$

b. $400,000 \div 8 = 50,000$

10. You multiplied a number by 6 and then divided by 5. The answer was 36,000.
    What was the number?

a. $36,000 \times 5 = 180,000$

b. $180,000 \div 6 = 30,000$

11. A = 38,000
    B = 4 x A
    C = A + B
    What number is C?

$B = 4 \times 38,000 = 152,000$

$C = 38,000 + 152,000 = 190,000$

12. M = 214,000
    N = 3 x M - 78,000
    What number is N?

a. $3 \times 214,000 = 642,000$

b. $642,000 - 78,000 = 564,000$

UNIT A TEST

1. How much money is pictured below?

a.
$4,000

b.
$20,000

c.
$300,000

d.
$213,000

e.
$301,000

2. Write the answer:

a. 4,000 + 2,000 = __6,000__
b. 3,000 + 6,000 = __9,000__
c. 2,000 + 8,000 = __10,000__
d. 9,000 + 1,000 = __10,000__
e. 8,000 + 6,000 = __14,000__
f. 7,000 + 5,000 = __12,000__

3. Add:

a.	b.	c.	d.
521,000	496,000	269,000	79,000
34,000	87,000	132,000	648,000
+ 142,000	+ 164,000	+ 69,000	+ 173,000
697,000	747,000	470,000	900,000

4. Write the answer:

a. 7,000 - 6,000 = __1,000__
b. 9,000 - 7,000 = __2,000__
c. 10,000 - 4,000 = __6,000__
d. 10,000 - 3,000 = __7,000__
e. 11,000 - 8,000 = __3,000__
f. 14,000 - 8,000 = __6,000__

5. Subtract:

a.	b.	c.	d.
968,000	547,000	840,000	900,000
- 427,000	- 489,000	- 276,000	- 148,000
541,000	058,000	564,000	752,000

Level 12

6. Write the answer:
   a. 5 x 7,000 = __35,000__
   b. 9 x 6,000 = __54,000__
   c. 6,000 x 5 = __30,000__
   d. 8,000 x 9 = __72,000__

7. Multiply:
   a. 8 x 79,000
   b. 36 x 19,000
   c. 25,000 x 24

   = 632,000
   = 684,000
   = 600,000

8. Write the answer:
   a. 45,000 ÷ 5 = __9,000__
   b. 20,000 ÷ 4 = __5,000__
   c. 56,000 ÷ 7 = __8,000__
   d. 49,000 ÷ 7 = __7,000__
   e. 72,000 ÷ 9 = __8,000__
   f. 27,000 ÷ 3 = __9,000__

9. Divide:
   a.
$$\frac{121,000}{4)\overline{484,000}}$$
   b.
$$\frac{047,000}{5)\overline{235,000}}$$
   c.
$$\frac{025,000}{8)\overline{200,000}}$$

   d.
$$\frac{009,000}{15)\overline{135,000}}$$
   $$\underline{135}$$
   e.
$$\frac{015,000}{26)\overline{390,000}}$$
   $$\underline{26}$$
   $$130$$
   $$\underline{130}$$
   f.
$$\frac{008,000}{123)\overline{984,000}}$$
   $$\underline{984}$$

10. A builder built 9 houses: 5 for $75,000 each and 4 for $69,000 each. How much did the project cost?

    a. 5 x $75,000 = $375,000
    b. 4 x $69,000 = $276,000
    c. Total Cost $651,000

11. A bank branch started with 4,000 five-dollar bills. During the day, $19,000 was deposited, and $28,000 was withdrawn by customers. How much money was in the bank at the end of the day?

    a. 4,000 x $5 = $20,000
    b. $20,000 + $19,000 = $39,000
    c. $39,000 - $28,000 = $11,000

12. Divide the sum of 49,000 and 131,000 by 12.

    a. 49,000 + 131,000 = 180,000
    b. 180,000 ÷ 12 = 15,000

13. You started with 35,000. You subtracted a number and then multiplied by 7. The answer was 168,000. What was the number?

    a. 168,000 ÷ 7 = 24,000
    b. 35,000 - 24,000 = 11,000

14. A = 3 x 7,000
    B = A + 9,000
    C = B - 5,000
    What number is C?

    A = 21,000
    B = 21,000 + 9,000 = 30,000
    C = 30,000 - 5,000 = 25,000

Date _____

How many dollars are pictured below?

- You may use boxes as shown to the right.
- The number presented is written 3,142 or 3142.
- It is read: three thousand one hundred forty-two

1,000'S	100'S	10'S	1'S
3	1	4	2

How many dollars are pictured below?

- Fill in the boxes.
- How is the numeral written? _2,030 or 2030._
- How is the number read? _two thousand thirty_

1,000'S	100'S	10'S	1'S
2	0	3	0

How many dollars are pictured below?

- Fill in the boxes.
- How is the numeral written? _1,032 or 1032._
- How is the numeral read? _one thousand thirty-two_

1,000'S	100'S	10'S	1'S
1	0	3	2

How many dollars are pictured below?

- Fill in the boxes.
- How is the numeral written? _2,003 or 2003._
- How is the numeral read? _two thousand three_

1,000'S	100'S	10'S	1'S
2	0	0	3

APPLICATIONS

1.	How many dollars are pictured?

a.

$2,100

b.

$3,020

c.

$1,002

2. In the numeral to the right: 3,972
   a. The 2 represents the number of   ones
   b. The 7 represents the number of   tens
   c. The 9 represents the number of   hundreds
   d. The 3 represents the number of   thousands

3. Write a numeral for:
   a. 8 thousands, 9 hundreds, 6 tens, and 7 ones.   8967
   b. 7 thousands, 5 tens, and 6 ones.   7056
   c. 3 thousands, 2 tens, and 9 ones.   3029
   d. 8 thousands and 4 tens.   8040
   e. 3 tens and 9 hundreds.   930
   f. 4 thousands and 3 ones.   4003

4. Write a numeral for:
   a. 7,000 + 500 + 30 + 9   7539
   b. 8,000 + 40   8040
   c. 9,000 + 8   9008
   d. 4,000 + 600   4600
   e. 1,000 + 30 + 7   1037
   f. 2,000 + 400 + 8   2408

Level 12

Date_____

7   ADDING

Example 1.

You want to add: 3014 + 2341 + 4323

Discussion:

You may also use boxes as shown to the right.

- Add ones: 8 ones
- Add tens: 7 tens
- Add hundreds: 6 hundreds
- Add thousands: 9 thousands

1,000'S	100'S	10'S	1'S
3	0	1	4
2	3	4	1
+ 4	3	2	3
9	6	7	8

The answer is ___9,678___

Example 2.

You want to do the addition to the right.

Discussion:

The procedure is, as you know, to add ones, then tens, then hundreds and then thousands; and whenever you have 10 or more in a certain column, you group.

- Add the ones: 24 ones

       24 ones = 2 tens and 4 ones
- Add the tens: 18 T's

      18 T's = 1 H and 8 T's
- Add the hundreds: 14 H's

      14 H's = 1 Th and 4 H's
- Add the thousands: 7 Th's

1,000'S	100'S	10'S	1'S
3	5	6	7
	1	8	6
+ 2	5	2	9
1	2	0	2
7	4	8	4

The answer is ___7,484___

You may, of course, do without the boxes.
Do the following additions:

a.	b.	c.	d.
1,204 903 + 4,589 **6,696**	987 4,008 + 3,909 **8,904**	1,808 4,764 + 458 **7,030**	4,543 915 + 2,542 **8,000**

e.	f.	g.	h.
2,341 1,152 203 + 4,200 **7,896**	1,394 1,486 2,625 1,784 + 2,698 **9,987**	1,542 014 2,173 1,727 1,814 + 130 **7,400**	145 1,274 5,011 532 1,028 + 1,010 **9,000**

Level 12   © Copyright by L. George Saad

Add:

a. 2,151 1,082 1,193 + 1,122 **5,548**	b. 1,513 2,219 1,102 + 3,014 **7,848**	c. 1,789 897 3,014 + 2,985 **8,685**	d. 5,842 1,235 938 + 764 **8,779**
e. 631 1,472 893 2,964 + 250 **6,210**	f. 1,789 113 1,234 2,412 + 360 **5,908**	g. 2,642 1,327 1,823 1,716 + 1,531 **9,039**	h. 1,152 1,276 2,784 1,514 + 1,274 **8,000**

B

APPLICATIONS

1. The figure to the right represents
   a piece of land.
   Find the perimeter (the distance
   around it). (dimensions are in yards)
   <u>**6,598 yd.**</u>

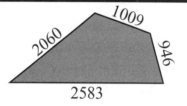

    1009
    2060
    2583
 + 946
    6598

2. A car dealer sold four cars for the
   prices shown.
   How much did he get for the four cars?
            <u>**$9,537**</u>

    $2,983
    $1,846
    $3,008
    $1,700

3. You subtracted 2,659 from a number.
   The answer was 3,948.
   What was the number? $2,659 + 3,948 = 6,607$

4. The difference between two numbers is 7,396.
   The smaller number is 1,006.
   What is the larger number? $7,396 + 1,006 = 8,402$

5. Add the sum of 2,954 and 1,396 to 4,008.   a. $2,954 + 1,396 = 4,350$
                                                  b. $4,008 + 4,350 = 8,358$

8 SUBTRACTING

Example 1.

You want to subtract: 9865 - 5213

	1,000'S	100'S	10'S	1'S
	9	8	6	5
-	5	2	1	3
	4	6	5	2

Discussion:
- Subtract ones: 5 ones - 3ones = 2 ones
- Subtract tens: 6 tens - 1 ten = 5 tens
- Subtract hundreds: 8 hundreds - 2 hundreds = 6 hundreds
- Subtract thousands: 9 thousands - 5 thousands = 4 thousands

Example 2.

Do the subtraction to the right.

	1,000'S	100'S	10'S	1'S
	6	3	9	5
-	2	6	8	2
	3	7	1	3

- 5 ones - 2 ones = 3 ones
- 9 tens - 8 tens = 1 ten
- 13 H's - 6 H's = 7 H's
- 5 Th's - 2Th's = 3 Th's

Example 3.

Do the subtraction to the right.

	1,000'S	100'S	10'S	1'S
	8	0	0	0
-	6	4	3	8
	1	5	6	2

- 10 ones - 8 ones = 2 ones
- 9 T's - 3 T's = 6 tens
- 9 H's - 4 H's = 5H's
- 7 Th's - 6 Th's = 1 Th

You may, of course, do without the boxes.
Do the following subtractions:

a.	8,453 - 2,421 **6,032**	b.	7,987 - 6,367 **1,620**	c.	7,165 - 1,879 **5,286**	d.	8,216 - 1,948 **6,268**
e.	8,900 - 3,465 **5,435**	f.	5,080 - 3,279 **1,801**	g.	9,040 - 6,289 **2,751**	h.	6,006 - 2,562 **3,444**
i.	8,001 - 3,068 **4,933**	j.	7,008 - 1,247 **5,761**	k.	9,000 - 3,765 **5,235**	l.	6,000 - 2,378 **3,622**

EXERCISES

Subtract:

a.	9,467 - 5,321 **4,146**	b.	8,358 - 1,972 **6,386**	c.	6,407 - 2,176 **4,231**	d.	9,870 - 3,289 **6,581**
e.	3,094 - 2,162 **932**	f.	5,089 - 4,327 **762**	g.	9,600 - 2,186 **7,414**	h.	8,400 - 1,715 **6,685**
i.	5,006 - 3,082 **1,924**	j.	7,009 - 6,423 **586**	k.	9,002 - 4,103 **4,899**	l.	6,001 - 2,418 **3,583**
m.	8,000 - 4,160 **3,840**	n.	9,000 - 3,750 **5,250**	o.	5,000 - 3,103 **1,897**	p.	7,000 - 2,168 **4,832**

APPLICATIONS

1. a. What number do you add to 1,798
    for the answer to be 4,000 ? $4,000 - 1,798 = 2,202$
    b. What number do you subtract from
    6,000 for the answer to be 4,605? $6,000 - 4,605 = 1,395$

2. a. You added 4,876 to a number.
    The answer was 5,000.
    What was the number? $5,000 - 4,876 = 124$
    b. You subtracted 4,876 from a number.
    The answer was 5,000.
    What was the number? $4,876 + 5,000 = 9,876$

3. The sum of two numbers is 5,678.
    One number is 3,765.
    What is the other number? $5,678 - 3,765 = 1,913$

4. The difference between two numbers is 2,004.
    The larger number is 7,000.
    What is the smaller number? $7,000 - 2,004 = 4,996$

5. The difference between two numbers is 2,004.
    The smaller number is 7,100.
    What is the larger number? $7,100 + 2,004 = 9,104$

Level 12

APPLICATIONS

1. Ted, Sue and Sam have $3,960 altogether.
   Ted has $1,250. Sam has $365 less than Ted.
   How much does Sue have?

   a. $1,250 - $365 = $885
   b. $1,250 + $885 = $2,135
   c. $3,960 - $2,135 = $1,825

2. During weekdays, a drug store sells
   235 newspapers daily.
   If 1,900 papers are sold during the 7
   days of the week, how many papers
   are sold on Sundays?

   a. 6 x 235 = 1,410
   b. 1,900 - 1,410 = 490

3. A dealer bought a car for $1,293.
   He spent $877 on repairs and
   then sold it for $2,650.
   How much profit did he make?

   a. $1,293 + $877 = $2,170
   b. $2,650 - $2,170 = $480

4. The figure to the right represents
   a piece of land. (dimensions are in yards)

   a. Find the perimeter.

   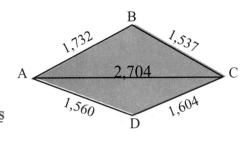

   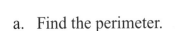
   1,732 + 1,537 + 1,604 + 1,560 = 6,433 yards

   b. You want to go from A to C. How
   much distance would you save if
   you take the shortcut instead
   of going through B?

   a. 1,732 + 1,537 = 3,269 yards
   b. 3,269 - 2,704 = 565 yards

B

5. a. You added a number to 2,718.
The answer was 6,000.
What was the number?   6,000 - 2,718 = 3,282

   b. You subtracted a number from 8,000.
The answer was 1,704.
What was the number?   8,000 - 1,704 = 6,296

   c. You subtracted 3,967 from a
number. The answer was 2,315.
What was the number?   2,315 + 3,967 = 6,282

6. You subtracted a number from
9,000, then added 1,384.
The answer was 7,358.   a. 7,358 - 1,384 = 5,974
What was the number?   b. 9,000 - 5,974 = 3,026

7. You added a number to 1,384 and
then subtracted 4,268.
The answer was 2,429.   a. 2,429 + 4,268 = 6,697
What was the number?   b. 6,697 - 1,384 = 5,313

8. A is 1,965, B is 1,378 more than A,
and C is 1,948 less than B.   a. B = 1,965 + 1,378 = 3,343
What number is C?   b. C = 3,343 - 1,948 = 1,395

9. Study the following equation:
N = (4 x 208) + (3 x 306)
What number is N?   N = 832 + 918 = 1,750

10. The sum of three numbers X, Y, and Z is 9,000.   a. 4,756 + 2,563 = 7,319
X is 4,756 and Z is 2,563. What number is Y?   b. 9,000 - 7,319 = 1,681

9 MULTIPLYING BY A ONE-DIGIT NUMERAL

Example 1.

You want to multiply: 2 x 2,314

Discussion:

You may use boxes:

	1,000'S	100'S	10'S	1'S	
2 x 2,314 =	4	6	2	8	= 4,628

- 2 x 4 ones = 8 ones
- 2 x 1 ten = 2 tens
- 2 x 3 hundreds = 6 hundreds
- 2 x 2 thousands = 4 thousands

Example 2.

Multiply: 3 x 2,564

Discussion:

You may use boxes:

	1,000'S	100'S	10'S	1'S	
3 x 2,564 =	7	6	9	2	= 7,692

- 3 x 4 ones = 12 ones
  12 ones = 2 ones + 1 ten
- 3 x 6 T's = 18 T's
  18 T's + 1 T = 19 T's
  19 T's = 1 H + 9 T's
- 3 x 5 H's = 15 H's
  15 H's + 1 H = 16 H's
  16 H's = 1 Th + 6 H's
- 3 x 2 Th's = 6 Th's
  6 Th's + 1 Th = 7 Th's

You can, of course, do without the boxes.

Do the following multiplications:

a. 3 x 2,364 =   __7,092__   b. 4 x 2,065 =   __8,260__

c. 6 x 1,008 =   __6,048__   d. 5 x 1,876 =   __9,380__

e. 2 x 4,098 =   __8,196__   f. 9 x 1,019 =   __9,171__

g. 3 x 3,309 =   __9,927__   h. 2 x 3,987 =   __7,974__

i. 4 x 2,076 =   __8,304__   j. 8 x 1,202 =   __9,616__

k.		l.		m.		n.	
	4,543		2,468		3,089		1,015
	x 2		x 4		x 3		x 8
	9,086		**9,872**		**9,267**		**8,120**

o.		p.		q.		r.	
	899		1,605		2,608		1,007
	x 8		x 6		x 3		x 5
	7,192		**9,630**		**7,824**		**5,035**

B

EXERCISES

Multiply:

1.

a. 2 x 1234 = ___2468___	b. 4 x 2121 = ___8484___	c. 8 x 1111 = ___8888___
d. 3 x 2103 = ___6309___	e. 5 x 1001 = ___5005___	f. 4 x 2002 = ___8008___
g. 3 x 1523 = ___4569___	h. 6 x 1311 = ___7866___	i. 7 x 1041 = ___7287___
j. 9 x 834 = ___7506___	k. 3 x 3015 = ___9045___	l. 4 x 2105 = ___8420___
m. 7 x 1024 = ___7168___	n. 9 x 1005 = ___9045___	o. 8 x 1051 = ___8408___

2.

a. 2123 x 3 = 6369	b. 923 x 8 = 7384	c. 1942 x 3 = 5826	d. 2194 x 4 = 8776
e. 1354 x 6 = 8124	f. 1294 x 7 = 9058	g. 785 x 9 = 7065	h. 494 x 8 = 3952
i. 2125 x 4 = 8500	j. 1065 x 6 = 6390	k. 1025 x 8 = 8200	l. 1404 x 5 = 7020

B

APPLICATIONS

1. One mile is 1760 yards.
   Point A is 4 miles and 890 yards
   away from point B.
   How far away is A from B in yards?

   a. 4 x 1760 = 7040
   b. 7040 + 890 = 7930

2. A drug store receives a shipment
   of 8,000 cards. 1205 boxes with
   6 cards in each box were sold.
   How many cards are still there?

   a. 1205 x 6 = 7230
   b. 8000 - 7230 = 770

3. Ted collects pennies and nickels.
   He has 1,958 pennies and 984 nickels.
   How much money does Ted have?

   a. 948 x 5¢ = 4740¢
   b. 4740¢ + 1958¢ = 6698¢
   = $66.98

4. You added a number to 3901 and
   then divided by 5. The answer
   was 878. What was the number?

   a. 878 x 5 = 4390
   b. 4390 - 3901 = 489

5. (3 x 1201) + (5 x 901) = A
   What number is A?

   3603 + 4505 = 8108

Level 12

10 MULTIPLYING BY TENS OR HUNDREDS

- Suppose you have 10 long strings, with 364 beads in each string.
  Below is a picture of a part of the arrangement.
  In all how many beads are there?

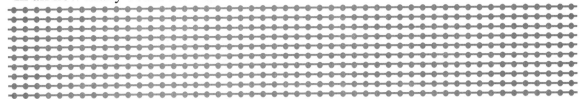

Discussion:

You may see the arrangement as ten 364's, or as 364 tens.

   364 x 10 = 364 tens = 3640

So, 10 x 364 = 364 tens = 3640

Similarly:

a. 248 x 10 = __2480__	b. 907 x 10 = __9070__	c. 10 x 630 = __6300__
10 x 248 = __2480__	10 x 907 = __9070__	630 x 10 = __6300__

B

- Suppose you have 20 long strings, with 364 beads in each string.
  Below is a picture of a part of the arrangement.
  In all, how many beads are there?

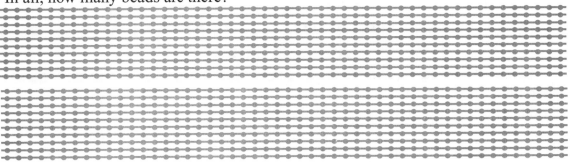

Discussion:

You may see the arrangement at twenty 364's or 364 twenties.

Also you may see 364 twenties as two 364 tens.

   364 x 20 = 2 x 364 tens = 728 tens = 7280

So, 20 x 364 = 2 x 364 tens = 728 tens = 7280

Similarly:

   a. 30 x 127 = 3 x 127 tens = 381 tens = 3810
       127 x 30 = 3 x 127 tens = 381 tens = 3810
   b. 40 x 236 = 4 x 236 tens = 944 tens = 9440
       236 x 40 = 4 x 236 tens = 944 tens = 9440

- You can, of course, multiply directly:

a. 80 x 124 = __9920__	b. 40 x 205 = __8200__	c. 60 x 150 = __9000__
124 x 80 = __9920__	205 x 40 = __8200__	150 x 60 = __9000__

Multiply:

1. a. 20 x 138 = ___2760___   b. 30 x 253 = ___7590___   c. 80 x 121 = ___9680___
   d. 60 x 132 = ___7920___   e. 20 x 416 = ___8320___   f. 40 x 243 = ___9720___
   g. 30 x 315 = ___9450___   h. 50 x 185 = ___9250___   i. 60 x 109 = ___6540___
   j. 80 x 112 = ___8960___   k. 40 x 178 = ___7120___   l. 70 x 118 = ___8260___
   m. 20 x 178 = ___3560___   n. 30 x 314 = ___9420___   o. 20 x 419 = ___8380___
   p. 40 x 215 = ___8600___   q. 50 x 198 = ___9900___   r. 80 x 102 = ___8160___

2. a. 317 x 20 = ___6340___   b. 220 x 40 = ___8800___   c. 317 x 30 = ___9510___
   d. 150 x 60 = ___9000___   e. 386 x 20 = ___7720___   f. 109 x 90 = ___9810___
   g. 428 x 20 = ___8560___   h. 107 x 80 = ___8560___   i. 214 x 40 = ___8560___
   j. 128 x 70 = ___8960___   k. 294 x 30 = ___8820___   l. 105 x 80 = ___8400___
   m. 178 x 50 = ___8900___   n. 105 x 60 = ___6300___   o. 225 x 40 = ___9000___
   p. 375 x 20 = ___7500___   q. 270 x 30 = ___8100___   r. 160 x 50 = ___8000___

B

APPLICATIONS

1. A bank teller has 40 fifty-dollar bills
    and 78 one hundred-dollar bills.
    How much money does she have?

    40 x $50 + 78 x $100
    = $2000 + $7800 = $9800

2. A truck driver drove 30 hours at an
    average speed of 50 miles per hour.
    How many miles did he drive?

    30 x 50 = 1500

3. In the supply room there were 20 boxes
    with 144 pencils in each box.
    Now there are 960 pencils.
    How many pencils were given to students?

    a. 20 x 144 = 2880
    b. 2880 - 960 = 1920

4. A is 1678 and B is 200 more than 3 times A.
    Find the sum of A and B.

    B = (3 x 1678) + 200
    B = 5034 + 200 = 5234
    A + B = 1678 + 5234 = 6912

5. Find the answer:
    a. (30 x 195) + (13 x 200)   b. (60 x 149) - (40 x 200)
        5850 + 2600 = 8450   8940 - 8000 = 940

37

11 MULTIPLYING BY A TWO OR THREE-DIGIT NUMERAL

Example.

In the store room there are 28 boxes, with 144 cards in each box.
In all, how many cards are there?

Discussion:

The situation calls for the multiplication: 28 x 144.
You get the answer in 3 steps:

- 8 x 144 = 1152
- 20 x 144 = 2880
- Add   4032

You also may do the work as shown to the right.

	144		144
	x 28	or	x 28
	1152		1152
	2880		288
	4032		4032

Do the following multiplications.

a.	103	b.	234	c.	128	d.	304
	x 25		x 35		x 35		x 32
	515		1170		640		608
	206		702		384		912
	2575		8190		4480		9728

EXERCISES

Multiply:

a.	58	b.	86	c.	14	d.	75
	x 29		x 17		x 27		x 35
	522		602		98		375
	116		86		28		225
	1682		1462		378		2625

e.	164	f.	293	g.	319	h.	225
	x 24		x 18		x 26		x 25
	656		2344		1914		1125
	328		293		638		450
	3936		5274		8294		5625

i.	309	j.	103	k.	201	l.	302
	x 29		x 23		x 29		x 24
	2781		309		1809		1208
	618		206		402		604
	8961		2369		5829		7248

APPLICATIONS

1. You have 35 quarters.
   How much money do you have?

   <u>35 x 25¢ = 875¢ = $8.75</u>

2. You need 18¢ more than you have
   in order to buy 24 pens at 29¢ each.
   How much money do you have?

   a. <u>24 x 29¢ = 696¢</u>
   b. <u>696¢ - 18¢ = 678¢ = $6.78</u>

3. One week, a farmer sold 128 dozen
   eggs. How many eggs did he sell?

   <u>128 x 12 = 1536</u>

4. On a vacation, a family drove 25 hours
   at a speed of 48 miles per hour.
   How many miles did the family drive?

   <u>25 x 48 = 1200</u>

5. John takes home $736 a month.
   He saves $1270 a year.
   How much does he spend in a year?

   a. <u>12 x $736 = $8832</u>
   b. <u>$8832 - $1270 = $7562</u>

6. You divide a number by 38.
   The answer was 79.
   What was the number?

   <u>38 x 79 = 3002</u>

7. Find the answer:

a. (48 x 105) - 2384	b. 7900 - (38 x 49)
<u>5040 - 2384 = 2656</u>	<u>7900 - 1862 = 6038</u>
c. (65 x 49) - (25 x 104)	d. (89 x 54) - (68 x 51)
<u>3185 - 2600 = 585</u>	<u>4806 - 3468 = 1338</u>

B

Level 12

12   DIVIDING BY A ONE-DIGIT NUMERAL

Example 1.
   Do the division to the right:
   - 6 Thousands ÷ 3 = 2 Thousands
   - 3 Hundreds ÷ 3 = 1 Hundred
   - 0 Tens ÷ 3 = 0 Tens
   - 9 Ones ÷ 3 = 3 Ones

$$\frac{2{,}103}{3)6{,}309}$$

Example 2.
   Do the division to the right:
   - 7 Th's ÷ 5 = 1 Th, and 2 Th's remain.
   - 23 H's ÷ 5 = 4 H's, and 3 H's remain.
   - 39 T's ÷ 5 = 7 T's, and 4 T's remain.
   - 45 Ones ÷ 5 = 9 Ones

$$\frac{1{,}479}{5)7{,}395}$$

B

EXERCISES

Divide:

a. $\dfrac{1{,}111}{7)7{,}777}$	b. $\dfrac{1{,}321}{3)3{,}963}$	c. $\dfrac{2{,}112}{4)8{,}448}$	d. $\dfrac{2{,}413}{2)4{,}826}$
e. $\dfrac{2{,}031}{3)6{,}093}$	f. $\dfrac{2{,}001}{4)8{,}004}$	g. $\dfrac{1{,}001}{5)5{,}005}$	h. $\dfrac{4{,}213}{2)8{,}426}$
i. $\dfrac{1{,}624}{2)3{,}248}$	j. $\dfrac{1{,}915}{5)9{,}575}$	k. $\dfrac{1{,}127}{8)9{,}016}$	l. $\dfrac{1{,}618}{4)6{,}472}$
m. $\dfrac{1{,}033}{8)8{,}264}$	n. $\dfrac{1{,}067}{5)5{,}335}$	o. $\dfrac{0{,}906}{6)5{,}436}$	p. $\dfrac{0{,}302}{9)2{,}718}$
q. $\dfrac{950}{4)3{,}800}$	r. $\dfrac{3{,}017}{3)9{,}051}$	s. $\dfrac{901}{7)6{,}307}$	t. $\dfrac{1{,}060}{6)6{,}360}$
u. $\dfrac{1{,}699}{5)8{,}495}$	v. $\dfrac{2{,}092}{4)8{,}368}$	w. $\dfrac{2{,}098}{3)6{,}294}$	x. $\dfrac{375}{8)3{,}000}$

1. a. How many yards are in 7,002 feet?   a. $7,002 \div 3 = 2,334$

    b. How many gallons are in 8,176 pints?   b. $8,176 \div 8 = 1,022$

2. Tom had 7 boxes with 935 pennies in each box.
    He exchanged them for nickels.   a. $7 \times 935 = 6,545$
    How many nickels did he get?   b. $6,545 \div 5 = 1,309$

3. During 6 days, 3,042 individuals used
    the public library.
    What is the average number of individuals
    who used the library per day? $3,042 \div 6 = 507$

4. In 5 months Tom and his family covered
    8,735 miles.
    What is the average distance they
    covered monthly? $8,735 \div 5 = 1,747$ miles

5. You subtracted 3,872 from a number,
    and then multiplied by 4.
    The answer was 9,204.   a. $9,204 \div 4 = 2,301$
    What was the number?   b. $3,872 + 2,301 = 6,173$

6. You subtracted a number from 9,000
    and then multiplied by 3.
    The answer was 8,412.   a. $8,412 \div 3 = 2,804$
    What was the number?   b. $9,000 - 2,804 = 6,196$

7. You started with a number. You added
    2,398, then divided by 7.
    The answer was 853.   a. $853 \times 7 = 5,971$
    What was the number?   b. $5,971 - 2,398 = 3,573$

8. Study the following equation:
    $N = 9,000 - (9,010 \div 5)$

    What number is N? $N = 9,000 - 1,802 = 7,198$

B

41

13   ESTIMATING THE ANSWER

Example 1.
   In the division to the right,
   what is the answer?

$$\frac{004}{35)140}$$

Discussion:
- The answer is not 0.
  Why?   Because 0 x 35 = 0
- The answer is not 10.
  Why?   Because 10 x 35 = 350
- Is the answer 1, 2, 3, 4, 5, 6, 7, 8, or 9?   __4__

Example 2.
   In the division to the right,
   what is the answer?

$$\frac{009}{85)765}$$

Discussion:
- The answer is not 0.
  Why?   Because 0 x 85 = 0
- The answer is not 10.
  Why?   Because 10 x 85 = 850
- Is the answer 1, 2, 3, 4, 5, 6, 7, 8, or 9?   __9__

EXERCISES

Divide:

a. $\frac{005}{57)285}$ $\underline{285}$	b. $\frac{009}{79)711}$ $\underline{711}$	c. $\frac{008}{96)768}$ $\underline{768}$	d. $\frac{005}{138)690}$ $\underline{690}$
e. $\frac{004}{238)952}$ $\underline{952}$	f. $\frac{003}{584)1,752}$ $\underline{1752}$	g. $\frac{005}{624)3,120}$ $\underline{3,120}$	h. $\frac{004}{415)1,660}$ $\underline{1,660}$
i. $\frac{009}{603)5,427}$ $\underline{5,427}$	j. $\frac{008}{248)1,984}$ $\underline{1,984}$	k. $\frac{005}{515)2,575}$ $\underline{2,575}$	l. $\frac{006}{316)1,896}$ $\underline{1,896}$
m. $\frac{007}{309)2,163}$ $\underline{2,163}$	n. $\frac{009}{717)6,453}$ $\underline{6,453}$	o. $\frac{007}{410)2,870}$ $\underline{2,870}$	p. $\frac{009}{190)1,710}$ $\underline{1,710}$

B

Level 12

As you divide, there may be a remainder as shown:

a.	b.	c.
$$\begin{array}{r}005\\85\overline{)498}\\ \underline{425}\\73\end{array}$$	$$\begin{array}{r}0\ 003\\392\overline{)1,248}\\ \underline{1,176}\\72\end{array}$$	$$\begin{array}{r}0\ 008\\350\overline{)2,924}\\ \underline{2,800}\\124\end{array}$$
The answer is 5, R73	The answer is ___3, R72___	The answer is ___8, R124___

EXERCISES

Divide:

a.	b.	c.	d.
$$\begin{array}{r}005\\74\overline{)435}\\ \underline{370}\\65\end{array}$$	$$\begin{array}{r}005\\98\overline{)568}\\ \underline{490}\\78\end{array}$$	$$\begin{array}{r}005\\39\overline{)204}\\ \underline{195}\\9\end{array}$$	$$\begin{array}{r}006\\46\overline{)289}\\ \underline{276}\\13\end{array}$$
e.	**f.**	**g.**	**h.**
$$\begin{array}{r}008\\75\overline{)605}\\ \underline{600}\\5\end{array}$$	$$\begin{array}{r}006\\125\overline{)797}\\ \underline{750}\\47\end{array}$$	$$\begin{array}{r}007\\158\overline{)1,158}\\ \underline{1,106}\\52\end{array}$$	$$\begin{array}{r}004\\512\overline{)2,176}\\ \underline{2,048}\\128\end{array}$$
i.	**j.**	**k.**	**l.**
$$\begin{array}{r}007\\450\overline{)3,158}\\ \underline{3,150}\\8\end{array}$$	$$\begin{array}{r}005\\294\overline{)1,674}\\ \underline{1,470}\\204\end{array}$$	$$\begin{array}{r}009\\604\overline{)5,894}\\ \underline{5,436}\\458\end{array}$$	$$\begin{array}{r}006\\560\overline{)3,548}\\ \underline{3,360}\\188\end{array}$$
m.	**n.**	**o.**	**p.**
$$\begin{array}{r}003\\790\overline{)2,891}\\ \underline{2,370}\\521\end{array}$$	$$\begin{array}{r}002\\890\overline{)2,148}\\ \underline{1,780}\\368\end{array}$$	$$\begin{array}{r}007\\298\overline{)2,156}\\ \underline{2,086}\\70\end{array}$$	$$\begin{array}{r}009\\428\overline{)4,164}\\ \underline{3,852}\\312\end{array}$$
q.	**r.**	**s.**	**t.**
$$\begin{array}{r}005\\565\overline{)2,948}\\ \underline{2,825}\\123\end{array}$$	$$\begin{array}{r}003\\584\overline{)2,000}\\ \underline{1,752}\\248\end{array}$$	$$\begin{array}{r}007\\970\overline{)6,940}\\ \underline{6,790}\\150\end{array}$$	$$\begin{array}{r}007\\381\overline{)2,680}\\ \underline{2,667}\\13\end{array}$$

B

Level 12

14 DIVIDING BY A TWO OR THREE-DIGIT NUMERAL

Example 1.

Do the division to the right.

Step by step:

- 1 Th ÷ 25 = 0 Th, 1 Th remains.
- 13 H's ÷ 25 = 0 H's, 13 H's remain.
- 132 T's ÷ 25 = 5 T's, 7 T's remain.
- 75 Ones ÷ 25 = 3 Ones.

```
     0053
25) 1325
    1250
      75
      75
```

Example 2.

Do the division to the right.

Step by step:

- 9Th's ÷ 248 = 0 Th, 9 Th's remain.
- 91 H's ÷ 248 = 0 H's, 91 H's remain.
- 917T's ÷ 248 = 3 T's, 173 T's remain.
- 1736 ones ÷ 248 = 7 ones.

```
      0037
248) 9176
     7440
     1736
     1736
```

EXERCISES

Divide:

a. $\begin{array}{r} 0072 \\ 25)\overline{1800} \\ 175 \\ 50 \\ 50 \end{array}$	b. $\begin{array}{r} 0014 \\ 76)\overline{1064} \\ 760 \\ 304 \\ 304 \end{array}$	c. $\begin{array}{r} 0064 \\ 125)\overline{8000} \\ 750 \\ 500 \\ 500 \end{array}$	d. $\begin{array}{r} 0012 \\ 86)\overline{1032} \\ 86 \\ 172 \\ 172 \end{array}$
e. $\begin{array}{r} 0037 \\ 89)\overline{3293} \\ 267 \\ 623 \\ 623 \end{array}$	f. $\begin{array}{r} 0046 \\ 130)\overline{5980} \\ 520 \\ 780 \\ 780 \end{array}$	g. $\begin{array}{r} 0028 \\ 75)\overline{2100} \\ 150 \\ 600 \\ 600 \end{array}$	h. $\begin{array}{r} 0052 \\ 170)\overline{8840} \\ 850 \\ 340 \\ 340 \end{array}$
i. $\begin{array}{r} 0024 \\ 126)\overline{3024} \\ 252 \\ 504 \\ 504 \end{array}$	j. $\begin{array}{r} 0037 \\ 245)\overline{9065} \\ 735 \\ 1715 \\ 1715 \end{array}$	k. $\begin{array}{r} 0015 \\ 418)\overline{6270} \\ 418 \\ 2090 \\ 2090 \end{array}$	l. $\begin{array}{r} 0026 \\ 315)\overline{8190} \\ 630 \\ 1890 \\ 1890 \end{array}$

Divide:

a.
```
      0155
25) 3875
      25
      137
      125
      125
      125
```

b.
```
      0541
12) 6492
      60
      49
      48
      12
      12
```

c.
```
      0226
35) 7910
      70
      91
      70
      210
      210
```

d.
```
      0315
26) 8190
      78
      39
      26
      130
      130
```

e.
```
      182
32) 5824
      32
      262
      256
      64
      64
```

f.
```
      216
45) 9720
      90
      72
      45
      270
      270
```

g.
```
      0049
28) 1372
      112
      252
      252
```

h.
```
      0041
64) 2624
      256
      64
      64
```

i.
```
      0064
57) 3648
      342
      228
      228
```

j.
```
      0025
125) 3125
      250
      625
      625
```

k.
```
      0016
225) 3600
      225
      1350
      1350
```

l.
```
      0028
125) 3500
      250
      1000
      1000
```

m.
```
      0025
368) 9342
      736
      1982
      1840
      142
```

n.
```
      0036
138) 5000
      4140
      860
      828
      32
```

o.
```
      0064
125) 8010
      7500
      510
      500
      10
```

p.
```
      0022
251) 5684
      502
      664
      502
      162
```

B

The following divisions need special attention:

a.	b.	c.	d.
0040 78) 3120 312	0030 69) 2070 207	0060 84) 5040 504	0060 145) 8700 870

e.	f.	g.	h.
200 43) 8627 86 27	300 25) 7512 75 12	200 39) 7815 78 15	0400 23) 9200 92

i.	j.	k.	l.
170 45) 7650 45 315 315	0270 24) 6480 48 168 168	120 26) 3120 26 52 52	150 32) 4800 32 160 160

m.	n.	o.	p.
0105 37) 3885 37 185 185	0301 25) 7525 75 25 25	0305 26) 7930 78 130 130	204 46) 9384 92 184 184

q.	r.	s.	t.
40 127) 5094 508 14	0400 24) 9617 96 17	0140 28) 3920 28 112 112	0209 35) 7340 70 340 315 25

46

1. a. You want to divide 3490 items into
   sets with 125 items in each set.
   What is the result?

   <u>27 sets are made and 115 items remain</u>

   b. You want to divide 3490 items equally
   into 125 sets.
   What is the result?

   <u>27 items in each set and 115 items remain</u>

   $$\begin{array}{r} 27 \\ 125 \overline{)\, 3490} \\ 250 \\ \hline 990 \\ 875 \\ \hline 115 \end{array}$$

2. Mr. Hills has 250 dozens of eggs,
   in boxes with 75 eggs in each box.
   How many boxes has he used?

   a. <u>250 x 12 = 3000</u>
   b. <u>3000 ÷ 75 = 40</u>

B

3. a. How many quarters do you
   exchange for 190 dimes?

   a. <u>190 x 10 = 1900</u>
   b. <u>1900 ÷ 25 = 76</u>

   b. How many dimes do you
   exchange for 180 quarters?

   a. <u>180 x 25 = 4500</u>
   b. <u>4500 ÷ 10 = 450</u>

4. a. You multiplied a number by 54.
   The answer was 4806.
   What was the number?

   $$\begin{array}{r} 0089 \\ 54 \overline{)\, 4806} \\ 432 \\ \hline 486 \\ 486 \\ \hline \end{array}$$

   b. 128 times N is 3200.
   What number is N?

   $$\begin{array}{r} 0025 \\ 128 \overline{)\, 3200} \\ 256 \\ \hline 640 \\ 640 \\ \hline \end{array}$$

5. What number do you add to the sum of
   1940 and 2760 to make it divisible by 39?   <u>19</u>

   $$\begin{array}{r} 0120 \\ 39 \overline{)\, 4700} \\ 39 \\ \hline 80 \\ 78 \\ \hline 20 \end{array}$$

15   WHAT IS THE NUMBER?

1. a. You added 5,342 to a number. The answer was 8,001. What was the number?

   $8{,}001 - 5{,}342 = 2{,}659$

   b. You added a number to 1,432. The answer was 4,090. What was the number?

   $4{,}090 - 1{,}432 = 2{,}658$

2. a. You subtracted a number from 5,000. The answer was 2,306. What was the number?

   $5{,}000 - 2{,}306 = 2{,}694$

   b. You subtracted 3,504 from a number. The answer was 2,967. What was the number?

   $3{,}504 + 2{,}967 = 6{,}471$

3. a. You multiplied a number by 27. The answer was 3348. What was the number?

   ```
       0124
   27) 3348
       27
       64
       54
      108
      108
   ```

   b. You multiplied 38 by a number. The answer was 2470 What was the number?

   ```
        0065
   38) 2470
       228
       190
       190
   ```

4. a. You divided a number by 25. The answer was 125. What was the number?

   ```
       125
   x    25
       625
       250
      3125
   ```

   b. You divided 3250 by a number. The answer was 125. What was the number?

   ```
         0026
   125) 3250
        250
        750
        750
   ```

5. a. You divided a number by 36. The answer was 59 and a remainder of 26. What was the number?

   a. $36 \times 59 = 2124$
   b. $2124 + 26 = 2150$

   b. You divided 5420 by a number. The answer was 60 and a remainder of 20. What was the number?

   a. $5420 - 20 = 5400$
   b. $5400 \div 60 = 90$

6. The sum of 98 and N is 3409.
   What number is N?

   3409 - 98 = 3311

7. The product of 68 and X is 2516.
   What number is X?

   $$\begin{array}{r} 0037 \\ 68{\overline{\smash{\big)}\,2516}} \\ \underline{204} \\ 476 \\ \underline{476} \end{array}$$

8. In a division, the dividend is 3000.
   and the quotient is 75.
   What was the divisor?

   $$\begin{array}{r} 0040 \\ 75{\overline{\smash{\big)}\,3000}} \\ \underline{3000} \end{array}$$

9. In a division, the divisor is 65, and
   the answer is 24 and a remainder of 18.
   What is the dividend?

   a. 65 x 24 = 1560
   b. 1560 + 18 = 1578

10. The difference between 2010 and A is 1070.
    There are two values for A.
    What are they?

    2010 + 1070 = 3080
    or 2010 - 1070 = 940

11. a. What is the smallest number you
       subtract from 9753 to make the
       number divisible by 25?
    b. What is the smallest number you add
       to 9753 to make the answer divisible by 25?

    3

    22

    $$\begin{array}{r} 0390 \\ 25{\overline{\smash{\big)}\,9753}} \\ \underline{75} \\ 225 \\ \underline{225} \\ 3 \end{array}$$

12. N - (10 x 300) = 4000
    What number is N?

    a. N - 3000 = 4000
    b. N = 4000 + 3000 = 7000

13. A + (20 x 400) = 9000
    What number is A?

    a. A + 8000 = 9000
    b. A = 9000 - 8000 = 1000

14. You multiplied a number by 25, and then
    added 3000. The answer was 7000.
    What was the number?

    a. 7000 - 3000 = 4000
    b. 4000 ÷ 25 = 160

15. You added 1728 to a number and then
    divided by 25. The answer was 364.
    What was the number?

    a. 364 x 25 = 9100
    b. 9100 - 1728 = 7372

B

WHAT IS THE NUMBER?

1. a. You multiplied a number by 25.
        The answer was 375.
        What was the number?

        ```
          015
        25) 375
            25
           125
           125
        ```

    b. You divided a number by 25.
        The answer was 375.
        What was the number?

        ```
          375
        x  25
         1875
          750
         9375
        ```

2. a. The sum of two numbers is 3850.
        One number is 35.
        What is the other number?

        ```
         3850
        -  35
         3815
        ```

    b. The product of two numbers is 3850.
        One number is 35.
        What is the other number?

        ```
          0110
        35)3850
           35
           35
           35
        ```

3. a. The difference between 2768 and
        a larger number is 2648.
        What is the number?

        ```
         2768
        +2648
         5416
        ```

    b. The difference between 2768 and
        a smaller number is 2648.
        What is the number?

        ```
         2768
        -2648
          120
        ```

4. a. What number do you add to 7678
        for the answer to be 9000?

        ```
         9000
        -7678
         1322
        ```

    b. What number do you subtract from
        6125 for the answer to be 5694?

        ```
         6125
        -5694
          431
        ```

5. a. In the division to the right,
        what number is missing?

        ```
                 0039
          238  238)
        x  39
         2142
          714
         9282
        ```

    b. In the division to the right,
        what number is missing?

        ```
           0122
         )9272
          0076
        122)9272
           854
           732
           732
        ```

6. The sum of 1837, 2634, and N is 7000.
   What number is N?

   a. $1837 + 2634 = 4471$
   b. $7000 - 4471 = 2529$

7. You multiplied a number by 25, and then
   added 2368. The answer was 7143.
   What was the number?

   a. $7143 - 2368 = 4775$
   b. $4775 \div 25 = 191$

8. You divided a number by 239.
   There was a remainder.
   a. What is the lowest number the remainder may be? ___1___
   b. What is the highest number the remainder may be? ___238___

9. You multiplied a number by 24,
   and then multiplied by 12.
   The answer was 4320.
   What was the number?

   a. $4320 \div 12 = 360$
   b. $360 \div 24 = 15$

10. You divided a number by 49, and
    then multiplied the quotient by 34.
    The answer was 3060.
    What was the number?

    a. $3060 \div 34 = 90$
    b. $90 \times 49 = 4100$

11. $N - 3000 = 70 \times 40$
    What number is N?

    a. $N - 3000 = 2800$
    b. $N = 2800 + 3000 = 5800$

12. $9000 - X = 18 \times 500$
    What number is X?

    a. $9000 - X = 9000$
    b. $X = 9000 - 9000 = 0$

B

WHAT IS THE NUMBER?

1. The sum of 1387 and N is 6000.
   What number is N?

   $N = 6000 - 1387 = 4613$

2. The sum of 3879, 2412, and A is 9048.
   What number is A?

   a. $3879 + 2412 = 6291$
   b. $9048 - 6291 = 2757$

3. $A = 25 \times 38$
   $B = 36 \times 49$
   What number is the sum of A and B?

   a. $A = 950$
   b. $B = 1764$
   c. $A + B = 2714$

4. $M = 7500 \div 25$
   $N = 3800 \div 190$
   What is the product of M and N?

   a. $M = 7500 \div 25 = 300$
   b. $N = 3800 \div 190 = 20$
   c. $M \times N = 300 \times 20 = 6000$

5. M, N, and T are three numbers.
   Given that M is 3978, N is 2000 less than
   M, and T is 1804 more than N.
   a. What number is N?

   $N = 3978 - 2000 = 1978$

   b. What number is T?

   $T = 1978 + 1804 = 3782$

6. a. 100 x a number = 8000
   What is the number?

   a. $8000 \div 100 = 80$

   b. A number x 10 = 7500
   What is the number?

   b. $7500 \div 10 = 750$

7. a. $3500 \div N = 70$
   What number is N?

   $N = 3500 \div 70 = 50$

   b. $X \div 56 = 24$
   What number is X?

   $X = 56 \times 24 = 1344$

8. You added 3700 to twice a number.
   The answer was 6000.
   What was the number?

   a. $6000 - 3700 = 2300$
   b. $2300 \div 2 = 1150$

9. You subtracted 2600 from 3 times a number.
The answer was 7000.
What was the number?

a. $7000 + 2600 = 9600$
b. $9600 \div 3 = 3200$

10. a. What number do you subtract from 8984 for the answer to be divisible by 125?
b. What number do you add to 8984 for the answer to be divisible by 125?

109

16

$$\begin{array}{r} 0071 \\ 125\overline{)8984} \\ \underline{875} \\ 234 \\ \underline{125} \\ 109 \end{array}$$

11. You added the product of 27 and 65 to 1796.
What was the answer?

a. $27 \times 65 = 1755$
b. $1755 + 1796 = 3551$

12. $N + (75 \times 38) = 6000$
What number is N?

a. $N + 2850 = 6000$
b. $N = 6000 + 2850 = 3150$

13. $X - (36 \times 49) = 1000$
What number is X?

a. $X - 1764 = 1000$
b. $X = 1764 + 1000 = 2764$

14. $(3 \times A) + 7000 = 9700$
What number is A?

a. $(3 \times A) = 9700 - 7000 = 2700$
b. $A = 2700 \div 3 = 900$

15. $(5 \times B) - 1500 = 2400$
What number is B?

a. $(5 \times B) = 2400 + 1500 = 3900$
b. $B = 3900 \div 5 = 780$

B

Date _____

1. How much money is pictured below?

_____$2,103_____

_____$1,002_____

2. Write numerals for:
   a. 3 Th's, 6 H's, 5 T's, and 8 ones _____3658_____
   b. 6 Th's, and 7 ones _____6007_____
   c. 4 Th's, and 3 tens _____4030_____
   d. 2 Th's, and 9 H's _____2900_____

3. Add:

a. 3,214	b. 1,761	c. 1,389	d. 2,157
1,602	2,902	2,678	1,292
1,151	1,613	1,984	1,346
+ 2,012	+ 1,423	+ 1,815	1,525
7,979	7,699	7,866	+ 1,680
			8,000

4. Subtract:

a. 5,083	b. 6,008	c. 7,005	d. 9,000
- 2,529	- 4,872	- 3,209	- 3,584
2,554	1,136	3,796	5,416

5. Ted had $3,925. Dan has $765 more than Ted. How much do they both have altogether?

   a. $3,925 + $765 = $4,690
   b. $4,690 + $3,925 = $8,615

6. A dealer bought two cars, one for $2,475 and the other for $3,150. He sold each car for $3,025.
   a. How much did he make on the first car? _____$3,025 - $2,475 = $550_____
   b. How much did he lose on the second car? _____$3,150 - $3,025 = $125_____

7. The difference between 968 and a larger number N is 1,697. Find the sum of the two numbers.

   a. N = 968 + 1,697 = 2,665
   b. 2,665 + 968 = 3,633

8. Fill in the boxes:

1,000'S	100'S	10'S	1'S

$3 \times 1,784 =$

5	3	5	2

9. Multiply:
   a. $2 \times 2,134 =$ __4,268__   b. $6 \times 1,312 =$ __7,872__
   c. $5 \times 1,241 =$ __6,205__   d. $8 \times 1,125 =$ __9,000__

e.	f.	g.
985	2,148	1,059
x 9	x 4	x 8
8,865	8,592	8,472

10. Multiply:
   a. $10 \times 764 =$ __7640__   b. $968 \times 10 =$ __9680__
   c. $20 \times 397 =$ __7940__   d. $148 \times 60 =$ __8880__
   e. $50 \times 196 =$ __9800__   f. $225 \times 40 =$ __9000__

11. Multiply:

a.	b.	c.
49	36	125
x 67	x 59	x 58
343	324	1000
294	180	625
3283	2124	7250

12. A builder bought 4 pieces of land
    for $1,975 each, and sold them
    all for $9,500.
    How much profit did he make?

    a. $4 \times \$1,975 = \$7,900$
    b. $\$9,500 - \$7,900 = \$1,600$

13. In the supply room, there are 20 boxes with
    48 crayons in each box, and 30 boxes with
    25 crayons in each box.
    How many crayons are there?

    a. $20 \times 48 = 960$
    b. $30 \times 25 = 750$
    c. Total $= 1,710$

14. You had 23 boxes with 96 stamps in each box.
    You sold 1293 stamps.
    How many stamps do you have left?

    a. $23 \times 96 = 2,208$
    b. $2,208 - 1,293 = 915$

15. $A + 7,000 = 20 \times 460$
    What number is A?

    a. $A + 7,000 = 9,200$
    b. $A = 9,200 - 7,000 = 2,200$

B

Level 12

16. Divide:

a. $9,369 \div 3 =$ ___3,123___

b. $7,842 \div 2 =$ ___3,921___

c. $3,052 \div 4 =$ ___763___

d. $9,005 \div 5 =$ ___1,801___

e. $3,094 \div 7 =$ ___442___

f. $6,012 \div 8 =$ ___751 R4___

g.
$$\begin{array}{r} 3,102 \\ \hline 3)9,306 \end{array}$$

h.
$$\begin{array}{r} 1,585 \\ \hline 5)7,925 \end{array}$$

i.
$$\begin{array}{r} 807 \text{ R1} \\ \hline 7)5,650 \end{array}$$

17. Divide:

a.
$$\begin{array}{r} 0005 \\ \hline 425)\,2125 \\ 2125 \end{array}$$

b.
$$\begin{array}{r} 0006 \\ \hline 273)\,1671 \\ 1638 \\ \hline 33 \end{array}$$

c.
$$\begin{array}{r} 0003 \\ \hline 932)\,2850 \\ 2796 \\ \hline 54 \end{array}$$

18. Divide:

a.
$$\begin{array}{r} 0023 \\ \hline 45)\,1035 \\ 90 \\ \hline 135 \\ 135 \end{array}$$

b.
$$\begin{array}{r} 0055 \\ \hline 125)\,6925 \\ 625 \\ \hline 675 \\ 625 \\ \hline 50 \end{array}$$

c.
$$\begin{array}{r} 0306 \\ \hline 25)\,7650 \\ 750 \\ \hline 150 \\ 150 \end{array}$$

19. a.   You had 3600 stamps.
You divided them equally into 45 sets.
What was the result?

$$\begin{array}{r} 0080 \\ \hline 45)\,3600 \\ 360 \end{array}$$

___80 stamps in each set___

b.   You had 2100 stamps.
You made them into sets with 14 stamps
in each set.
What was the result?

$$\begin{array}{r} 0150 \\ \hline 14)\,2100 \\ 14 \\ \hline 70 \\ 70 \end{array}$$

___150 sets were made___

20. For a concert, 234 tickets were
sold for the total price of $3510.
How much was the price of 1 ticket?

$$\begin{array}{r} 0015 \\ \hline 234)\,3510 \\ 234 \\ \hline 1170 \\ 1170 \end{array}$$

21. How many quarters do you get for 360 dimes?

a. $360 \times 10 = 3600$

b. $3600 \div 25 = 144$

22. a. The sum of A and 3,984 is 9,000.
        What number is A? $9,000 - 3,984 = 5,016$

    b. The product of 38 and another number
        is 1,900. What is the number? $1900 ÷ 38 = 50$

23. a. The difference between 2,008 and
        a smaller number X is 1,394.
        What number is X? $2,008 - 1,394 = 614$

    b. The difference between 3,084 and
        a larger number N is 2,648.
        What number is N? $3,084 + 2,648 = 5,732$

24. a. In a division, the divisor is 73, and
        the quotient is 34.
        What is the dividend? $73 × 34 = 2482$

    b. In a division, the divisor is 56, the
        quotient is 23, and the remainder is 15.   a. $56 × 23 = 1288$
        What is the dividend?   b. $1288 + 15 = 1303$

    c. In a division, the dividend is 2,015, the
        quotient is 80, and the remainder is 15.   a. $2015 - 15 = 2000$
        What is the divisor?   b. $2000 ÷ 80 = 25$

25. a. What number do you subtract from 1600
        for the answer to be divisible by 85?

    b. What number do you add to 1600
        for the answer to be divisible by 85?

$$\begin{array}{r} 0018 \\ 85\overline{)1600} \\ 85 \\ \hline 750 \\ 680 \\ \hline 70 \end{array}$$

70

15

26. You multiplied a number by 28, and
    then added 29. The answer was 3529.   a. $3529 - 29 = 3500$
    What was the number?   b. $3500 ÷ 28 = 125$

Level 12

- Numeral A is read,
  "three hundred ninety-seven"

ONES		
100'S	10'S	1'S
3	9	7

A

- Number B is read,
  "two hundred eighty-six thousands"

THOUSANDS		
100'S	10'S	1'S
2	8	6

B

- If you add the two numbers, a six-place number is created. It is read, "two hundred eighty-six thousand three hundred ninety-seven.", and is written 286,397

THOUSANDS			ONES		
100'S	10'S	1'S	100'S	10'S	1'S
2	8	6	3	9	7

- 286,397 is the same as:
  200,000 + 80,000 + 6,000 + 300 + 90 + 7

Similarly:

    a. 542,368 = 500,000 + 40,000 + 2,000 + 300 + 60 + 8

    b. 206,795 = 200,000 + 6,000 + 700 + 90 + 5

    c. 980,243 = _900,000 + 80,000 + 200 + 40 + 3_

    d. 490,005 = _400,000 + 90,000 + 5_

    e. 100,076 = _100,000 + 70 + 6_

- You know that the value of a digit depends on the place it occupies in the numeral.

Example 1.

In the numeral 428,576:

THOUSANDS			ONES		
100'S	10'S	1'S	100'S	10'S	1'S
4	2	8	5	7	6

- the 7 has a value of 7 tens.
- the 2 has a value of 2 tens of thousands.
- the 5 has a value of 5 hundreds.
- the 4 has a value of 4 hundreds of thousands.
- the 8 has a value of 8 thousands.
- the 6 has a value of 6 ones.

Example 2.

In the numeral 629,078

- the 7 has a value of _7 tens_
- the 8 has a value of _8 ones_
- the 2 has a value of _2 tens of thousands_
- the 9 has a value of _9 thousands_
- the 6 has a value of _6 hundreds of thousands_

APPLICATIONS

1. Write numerals for:
    a. 5 tens, 3 thousands, 9 ones, 6 hundreds of thousands,
        8 hundreds.   603,859
    b. 7 thousands, 9 hundreds, 7 tens of thousands,
        8 ones.   77,908
    c. 6 hundreds of thousands, 8 hundreds.   600,800
    d. 9 tens of thousands, 7 ones.   90,007

2. Write numerals for:
    a. $800,000 + 90,000 + 6,000 + 700 + 50 + 4$ 896,754
    b. $7 + 80 + 400 + 9,000 + 60,000 + 100,000$ 169,487
    c. $600,000 + 9,000 + 800$ 609,800
    d. $100 + 100,000 + 1$ 100,101
    e. $3,000 + 30 + 300,000$ 303,030

3. a. What number is 600 more than 600,000?   600,600
    b. What number is 7 more than 274,000?   274,007
    c. What number is 35 more than 501,000?   501,035
    d. What number is 834 more than 834,000?   834,834

4. a. What is the largest 5 place number?   99,999
    b. What is the smallest 5 place number?   10,000
    c. What is the largest 6 place number?   999,999
    d. What is the smallest 6 place number?   100,000

5. a. Use the digits 8, 3, 2, 5, and 6 to form the largest
        number you can.   86,532
    b. Use the same digits to form the smallest
        number you can.   23,568

6. a. Use the digits 1, 2, 5, 0, 9 and 8 to form
        the largest number you can form.   985,210
    b. Use the digits 0, 8, 5, 3, 2 and 1 to form
        the smallest number you can form.   012,358

Level 12

17 ADDING AND SUBTRACTING

You know that to add a column of numbers, you add the digits in each column, starting with the ones.

You may also know that if the sum of the digits in any column is 10 or more, you must group.

Example:

- Add the ones: 19

  19 ones must be grouped into 1 ten and 9 ones.
- Add the tens: 7

  No grouping is involved.
- Add the hundreds: 18

  18 hundreds must be grouped into 1 Th and 8 H's
- Add the thousands: 26

  26 Th's must be grouped into 2 T's of Th's, and 6 Th's.
- Add the tens of thousands: 20

  20 T's of Th's must be grouped into 2 H's of Th's and 0T's of Th's
- Add the hundreds of thousands: 7

$$\begin{array}{r} 237,613 \\ 179,427 \\ 105,534 \\ +\ 184,305 \\ \hline 706,879 \end{array}$$

Do the following additions:

a.	b.	c.	d.
94,867	65,167	26,121	113,452
18,958	179,283	110,043	365,121
26,796	34,335	254,487	197,133
+ 45,847	+ 218,019	+ 81,149	+ 24,294
186,468	496,804	471,800	700,000

You know that to subtract a number from another, you start with the ones, then the tens, then the hundreds, … etc.

You also know that sometimes the subtraction involves exchanging.

Example:

- 11 ones - 7 ones = 4 ones
- 12 tens - 4 tens = 8 tens
- 15 H's - 9 H's = 6 H's
- 14 Th's - 8 Th's = 6 Th's
- 11 T's of Th's - 7 T's of Th's = 4 T's of Th's
- 8 H's of Th's - 3 H's of Th's = 5 H's of Th's

$$\begin{array}{r} 925,631 \\ -\ 378,947 \\ \hline 546,684 \end{array}$$

Do the following subtractions:

a.	b.	c.	d.
761,234	897,064	605,397	700,000
- 526,789	- 321,789	- 16,488	- 164,897
234,445	575,275	588,909	535,103

Add:

a. 213,416	b. 89,253	c. 55,758	d. 254,312
651,251	37,625	79,801	73,175
20,002	18,749	194,311	2,267
+ 10,010	+ 27,942	84,070	197,038
894,679	**173,569**	+ 52,050	+ 43,208
		465,990	**570,000**

Subtract:

a. 976,382	b. 865,437	c. 189,413	d. 345,373
- 243,361	- 182,356	- 72,167	- 167,985
733,021	**683,081**	**117,246**	**177,388**
e. 300,058	f. 700,009	g. 400,000	h. 800,000
- 18,729	- 364,265	- 213,805	- 296,712
281,329	**335,744**	**186,195**	**503,288**

APPLICATIONS

1. In a city there are 347,879 males,
   and 319,658 females.
   a. How many people live in the city? <u>667,537</u>
   b. How many males are there more than
      females? <u>28,221</u>

2. The profits made by a company in three
   consecutive years were as follows: 1st year: $395,276
                                         2nd year:$209,195
                                         3rd year: $190,486

   a. Find the total profits made in
      the three years. <u>$794,957</u>
   b. Find the difference between the highest and
      the lowest profits. <u>$204,790</u>

3. A + 71,284 = 94,867
   What number is A? <u>A = 23,583</u>

4. The sum of A, B, and C is 900,000.
   Given that A = 325,164 and B = 246,851,   <u>a. A + B = 572,015</u>
   what number is C? <u>b. C = 327,985</u>

C

18   MULTIPLYING

Do the following multiplications:

a.	10 x 29 =	_290_
	29 x 10 =	_290_
b.	100 x 23 =	_2,300_
	23 x 100 =	_2,300_

You use the same principle to multiply larger numbers by 10, 100, 1000, … etc.
Do the following examples:

a.	1000 x 29 =	_29,000_	b.	1000 x 759 =	_759,000_
	29 x 1000 =	_29,000_		759 x 1000 =	_759,000_
c.	100 x 2,438 =	_243,800_	d.	10 x 4,386 =	_43,860_
	2,438 x 100 =	_243,800_		4,386 x 10 =	_43,860_
e.	1,000 x 2,469 =	_2,469,000_	f.	1,000 x 3,470 =	_3,470,000_
	2,469 x 1,000 =	_2,469,000_		3,470 x 1,000 =	_3,470,000_

EXERCISE

Multiply:

1.						
	a.	100 x 34 =	_3,400_	b.	100 x 79 =	_7,900_
	c.	10 x 4,350 =	_43,500_	d.	1,000 x 67 =	_67,000_
	e.	100 x 346 =	_34,600_	f.	100 x 2,768 =	_276,800_
	g.	1,000 x 149 =	_149,000_	h.	10 x 45,896 =	_458,960_
	i.	10 x 37,569 =	_375,000_	j.	100 x 3,469 =	_346,900_
	k.	1,000 x 240 =	_240,000_	l.	100 x 280 =	_28,000_
	m.	100 x 3,100 =	_310,000_	n.	10 x 5,4000 =	_54,000_
	o.	1,000 x 260 =	_260,000_	p.	100 x 4,200 =	_420,000_

2.						
	a.	25 x 100 =	_2,500_	b.	56 x 100 =	_5,600_
	c.	5,409 x 10 =	_54,090_	d.	68 x 1,000 =	_68,000_
	e.	408 x 100 =	_40,800_	f.	4,306 x 100 =	_430,600_
	g.	253 x 1,000 =	_253,000_	h.	39,007 x 10 =	_390,070_
	i.	49,080 x 10 =	_490,800_	j.	1,097 x 100 =	_109,700_
	k.	320 x 1,000 =	_320,000_	l.	420 x 100 =	_42,000_
	m.	5,100 x 100 =	_510,000_	n.	4,700 x 10 =	_47,000_
	o.	360 x 1,000 =	_360,000_	p.	7,900 x 100 =	_790,000_

MULTIPLYING BY TENS, HUNDREDS, OR THOUSANDS

Do the following multiplications:

a.	20 x 40 =	800	b. 30 x 80 =	2,400
	20 x 46 =	920	30 x 87 =	2,610
c.	40 x 200 =	8,000	d. 200 x 40 =	8,000
	40 x 235 =	9,400	200 x 48 =	9,600

You use the same principle to multiply larger numbers by 10, 100, 1000, … etc.
Do the following examples.

a.	30 x 400 =	12,000	b. 90 x 700 =	63,000
	30 x 427 =	12,810	90 x 706 =	63,540
c.	300 x 80 =	24,000	d. 700 x 60 =	42,000
	300 x 89 =	26,700	700 x 69 =	48,300
e.	800 x 900 =	720,000	f. 500 x 800 =	400,000
	800 x 970 =	776,000	500 x 801 =	400,500
g.	500 x 830 =	415,000	h. 800 x 960 =	768,000
	500 x 831 =	415,500	800 x 976 =	780,800

EXERCISES

Multiply:

1.
a.	40 x 700 =	28,000	b. 900 x 50 =	45,000
c.	600 x 800 =	480,000	d. 7,000 x 30 =	210,000
e.	80 x 500 =	40,000	f. 90 x 800 =	72,000
g.	200 x 3,000 =	600,000	h. 400 x 500 =	200,000
i.	70 x 9,000 =	630,000	j. 6,000 x 90 =	540,000
k.	500 x 800 =	400,000	l. 60 x 5,000 =	300,000

2.
a.	30 x 280 =	8,400	b. 70 x 370 =	25,900
c.	900 x 307 =	276,300	d. 300 x 276 =	82,800
e.	90 x 4,368 =	393,120	f. 50 x 3,006 =	150,300
g.	60 x 6,008 =	360,480	h. 300 x 2,970 =	891,000
i.	80 x 4,505 =	360,400	j. 40 x 5,050 =	202,000
k.	900 x 1,008 =	907,200	l. 200 x 3,980 =	796,000

C

Level 12

Date _____

MULTIPLYING BY A ONE-DIGIT NUMERAL

- You know how to multiply a four-digit numeral by a one-digit numeral.
  Do the following examples:

			d.	2,536	e.	1,009	f.	1,125
a.	8 x 1,235 =	_9,880_		x 3		x 9		x 8
b.	4 x 2,016 =	_8,064_		7,608		9,081		9,000
c.	6 x 1,505 =	_9,030_						

- You can use the same principles in multiplying a 5-digit, 6-digit, or any
  other numeral by a one-digit numeral.

  You may use boxes:

THOUSANDS			ONES		
100'S	10'S	1'S	100'S	10'S	1'S
8	3	7	4	3	2

4 x 209,358 = [8 3 7 4 3 2] = 837,432

Or you may do without the boxes:

			d.	78,345	e.	246,015	f.	19,005
a.	3 x 29,364 =	_88,092_		x 8		x 4		x 5
b.	4 x 78,205 =	_312,820_		626,760		984,060		95,025
c.	9 x 107,308 =	_965,772_						

EXERCISES

Multiply:

1.
a.	3 x 72,546 =	_217,638_	b.	5 x 23,873 =	_119,365_
c.	2 x 50,568 =	_101,136_	d.	7 x 25,652 =	_179,564_
e.	6 x 76,278 =	_457,668_	f.	9 x 98,724 =	_888,516_
g.	8 x 40,009 =	_320,072_	h.	6 x 50,034 =	_300,204_
i.	9 x 30,001 =	_270,009_	j.	5 x 80,004 =	_400,020_

2.
a.	3 x 213,123 =	_639,369_	b.	2 x 124,341 =	_248,682_
c.	7 x 124,315 =	_870,205_	d.	4 x 215,327 =	_861,308_
e.	4 x 200,305 =	_801,220_	f.	9 x 100,002 =	_900,018_
g.	6 x 150,035 =	_900,210_	h.	5 x 108,036 =	_540,180_
i.	7 x 101,204 =	_708,428_	j.	3 x 200,307 =	_600,921_

3.
a. 67,384	b. 90,306	c. 30,002	d. 90,106
x 5	x 7	x 4	x 8
336,920	632,142	120,008	720,848

4.
a. 125,328	b. 309,205	c. 200,005	d. 107,604
x 7	x 3	x 4	x 8
877,296	927,615	800,020	860,832

MULTIPLYING BY A TWO OR THREE-DIGIT NUMERAL

Example 1.

You want to multiply: 35 x 489

Discussion:

You multiply step by step:

a. 5 x 489 =   2445

b. 30 x 489 =   14670

c. add: 17115

```
   489              489
 x  35            x  35
  2445    or      2445
 14670            1467
 17115           17115
```

Example 2.

You want to multiply: 235 x 489

Discussion:

You want to multiply step by step.

a. 5 x 489 =   2445

b. 30 x 489 =   14670

c. 200 x 489 =   97800

d. add: 114,915

```
    489             489
  x 235           x 235
   2445    or      2445
  14670            1467
  97800             987
 114,915          114,915
```

Example 3.

You want to multiply 308 x 697

Discussion:

You multiply step by step.

a. 8 x 697 =   5576

b. 300 x 697 =   209100

c. add: 214676

```
    697             679
  x 308           x 308
   5576    or      5576
 209100            2091
 214676           214676
```

Do the following multiplications:

a.	b.	c.	d.
158 x 39 1422 474 6162	296 x 57 2072 1480 16872	317 x 56 1902 1585 17752	819 x 25 4095 1638 20475
e.	**f.**	**g.**	**h.**
1368 x 23 4104 2736 31464	7259 x 47 50813 29036 341173	4328 x 26 25968 8656 112528	8604 x 36 51624 25812 309744

     Level 12

EXERCISES

Multiply:

a.	694	b.	325	c.	379	d.	294
	x 118		x 183		x 215		x 386
	5552		975		1895		1764
	694		2600		379		2352
	694		325		758		882
	81892		59475		81485		113484

e.	1289	f.	1108	g.	2949	h.	1680
	x 237		x 376		x 268		x 397
	9023		6648		23592		11760
	3867		7756		17694		15120
	2578		3324		5898		5040
	305493		416608		790332		666960

i.	2304	j.	5120	k.	6170	l.	3105
	x 298		x 145		x 112		x 317
	18432		25600		12340		21735
	20736		20480		6170		3105
	4608		5120		6170		9315
	686592		742400		691040		984285

m.	365	n.	656	o.	540	p.	705
	x 270		x 380		x 230		x 310
	2555		5248		1620		705
	730		1968		1080		2115
	98550		249280		124200		218550

q.	1250	r.	307	s.	225	t.	3702
	x 105		x 206		x 107		x 205
	6250		1842		1575		18510
	1250		614		225		7404
	131250		63242		24075		758910

C

APPLICATIONS

1. A builder built 8 houses for the total cost of $600,000.
   He sold the houses for $95,900 each.
   How much profit did he make?

   a. 8 x $95,900 = $767,200
   b. $767,200 - $600,000 = $167,200

2. A theater which has 1,575 seats was full for 25 consecutive shows.
   a. How many persons attended the shows?
   b. If the ticket cost $8, how much money was collected in all three shows?

   a. 25 x 1,575 = 39,375
   b. 39,375 x $8 = $315,000

3. A newspaper sells 125,125 copies daily during the week (Monday - Saturday), and 238,395 copies on Sunday.
   How many copies are sold all week?

   a. 6 x 125,125 = 750,750
   b. 750,750 + 238,395 = 989,145

4. A = 30 x 298 and B = 70 x 650
   Find the sum of A and B.
   Find the difference between A and B.

   a. A = 8,940 and B = 45,500
   b. A + B = 54,440
   c. B - A = 36,560

5. Find the answer:

a. 70,000 - (305 x 208)	b. (402 x 306) - 97,258
70,000 - 63,440 = 6,560	123,012 - 97,258 = 25,754
c. (39 x 415) + (68 x 229)	d. (109 x 306) - (95 x 207)
16,185 + 15,572 = 31,757	33,354 - 19,665 = 13,689

Level 12

Do the following divisions:

a.	b.	c.
$\dfrac{0921}{4)\,3684}$	$\dfrac{1357}{5)\,6785}$	$\dfrac{0908}{9)\,8176}$ **R4**

• You use the same procedure in dividing a 5-place, 6-place, or any other numeral by one-digit numeral.

Do the following divisions:

a.	b.	c.
$\dfrac{21992}{4)\,87968}$	$\dfrac{1071}{6)\,6426}$	$\dfrac{06790}{8)\,54324}$ **R4**
d.	e.	f.
$\dfrac{076088}{9)\,684792}$	$\dfrac{134705}{7)\,942935}$	$\dfrac{106090}{8)\,848725}$ **R5**

EXERCISES

Divide:

a.	b.	c.
$\dfrac{312123}{3)\,936369}$	$\dfrac{241132}{2)\,482264}$	$\dfrac{211121}{4)\,844484}$
d.	e.	f.
$\dfrac{192651}{5)\,963255}$	$\dfrac{291418}{3)\,874254}$	$\dfrac{050879}{6)\,305274}$
g.	h.	i.
$\dfrac{035066}{7)\,245468}$ **R6**	$\dfrac{192974}{5)\,964872}$ **R2**	$\dfrac{050132}{6)\,300795}$ **R3**
j.	k.	l.
$\dfrac{24047}{2)\,48094}$	$\dfrac{279024}{3)\,837072}$	$\dfrac{065015}{5)\,325075}$
m.	n.	o.
$\dfrac{120132}{7)\,840924}$	$\dfrac{160118}{6)\,960708}$	$\dfrac{120119}{8)\,960952}$
p.	q.	r.
$\dfrac{125009}{6)\,750058}$ **R4**	$\dfrac{065004}{8)\,520036}$ **R4**	$\dfrac{085002}{4)\,340009}$ **R1**

Do the following divisions:

a.	b.	c.
$\underline{0036}$	$\underline{0120}$	$\underline{0302}$
48)1728	75)9000	25)7550
$\underline{144}$	$\underline{75}$	$\underline{75}$
288	150	50
$\underline{288}$	$\underline{150}$	$\underline{50}$

You follow the same procedure in dividing a 5-place, 6-place, or any number by another number.

Do the following divisions:

a.	b.	c.
$\underline{00920}$	$\underline{00306}$	$\underline{003060}$
25) 23000	85) 26010	128) 391680
$\underline{225}$	$\underline{255}$	$\underline{384}$
50	510	768
$\underline{50}$	$\underline{510}$	$\underline{768}$

EXCERCISES

Divide:

a.	b.	c.
$\underline{00438}$	$\underline{00552}$	$\underline{00679}$
52) 22776	87) 48024	93) 63147
$\underline{208}$	$\underline{435}$	$\underline{558}$
197	452	734
$\underline{156}$	$\underline{435}$	$\underline{651}$
416	174	837
$\underline{416}$	$\underline{174}$	$\underline{837}$

d.	e.	f.
$\underline{005986}$	$\underline{003148}$	$\underline{007384}$
34) 203524	58) 182584	79) 583336
$\underline{170}$	$\underline{174}$	$\underline{553}$
335	85	303
$\underline{306}$	$\underline{58}$	$\underline{237}$
292	278	663
$\underline{272}$	$\underline{232}$	$\underline{632}$
204	464	316
$\underline{204}$	$\underline{464}$	$\underline{316}$

EXERCISES

Divide:

a. $\dfrac{00135}{125)16875}$ $\underline{125}$ 437 $\underline{375}$ 625 $\underline{625}$	b. $\dfrac{00348}{245)85260}$ $\underline{735}$ 1176 $\underline{980}$ 1960 $\underline{1960}$	c. $\dfrac{000425}{397)168725}$ $\underline{1588}$ 992 $\underline{794}$ 1985 $\underline{1985}$
d. $\dfrac{00026}{385)10010}$ $\underline{770}$ 2310 $\underline{2310}$	e. $\dfrac{000318}{1215)386370}$ $\underline{3645}$ 2187 $\underline{1215}$ 9720 $\underline{9720}$	f. $\dfrac{000356}{1173)417588}$ $\underline{3519}$ 6568 $\underline{5865}$ 7038 $\underline{7038}$
g. $\dfrac{00350}{65)22750}$ $\underline{195}$ 325 $\underline{325}$	h. $\dfrac{01700}{42)71400}$ $\underline{42}$ 294 $\underline{294}$	i. $\dfrac{00280}{138)38640}$ $\underline{276}$ 1104 $\underline{1104}$
j. $\dfrac{00708}{36)25488}$ $\underline{252}$ 288 $\underline{288}$	k. $\dfrac{00509}{72)36648}$ $\underline{360}$ 648 $\underline{648}$	l. $\dfrac{00105}{485)50925}$ $\underline{485}$ 2425 $\underline{2425}$
m. $\dfrac{01020}{42)42840}$ $\underline{42}$ 84 $\underline{84}$	n. $\dfrac{02003}{36)72108}$ $\underline{72}$ 108 $\underline{108}$	o. $\dfrac{001006}{127)127762}$ $\underline{127}$ 762 $\underline{762}$

APPLICATIONS

1. a. What number do you subtract from 38216 for the answer to be divisible by 125? ___91___

$$\begin{array}{r} 00305 \\ 125\overline{)38216} \\ \underline{375} \\ 716 \\ \underline{625} \\ 91 \\ \underline{91} \end{array}$$

   b. What number do you add to 38216 for the answer to be divisible by 125? ___34___

2. a. In the division to the right, what is the missing number?

$$\begin{array}{r} 01290 \\ 56\overline{)} \end{array}$$

   $56 \times 1290 = 72240$

   b. In the division to the right, what is the missing number?

$$\begin{array}{r} 009021 \\ \overline{)676575} \end{array}$$

   $676575 \div 9021 = 75$

3. $A = (50225 \div 245) + 2738$
    What number is A?

    a. $50225 \div 245 = 205$
    b. $205 + 2738 = 2943$

4. $24 \times N = 13920$
    What number is N?

    $N = 13920 \div 24 = 580$

5. You multiplied a number by 39 and then added 848. The answer was 23,000. What was the number?

    a. $23,000 - 848 = 22152$
    b. $22,152 \div 39 = 568$

6. $(2 \times A) + 3400 = 5800$
    What number is A?

    a. $2 \times A = 5800 - 3400 = 2400$
    b. $A = 2400 \div 2 = 1200$

Level 12

20 MILLIONS - BILLIONS - TRILLIONS

- 1,000 thousands is a million. It is written 1,000,000.

  In millions, you can count up to 999 million.

  You can write a 9-place numeral, such as the one shown below:

MILLIONS			THOUSANDS			ONES		
100'S	10'S	1'S	100'S	10'S	1'S	100'S	10'S	1'S
9	3	6	2	7	8	1	4	5

= 936,278,145

- 1,000 millions is a billion. It is written 1,000,000,000.

  In billions, you can count up to 999 billions.

  You can write a 12-place numeral such as the one shown below:

BILLIONS			MILLIONS			THOUSANDS			ONES		
100'S	10'S	1'S	100'S	10'S	1'S	100'S	10'S	1'S	100'S	10'S	1'S
1	9	4	2	0	6	3	7	8	5	0	0

= 194,206,378,500

- 1,000 billions make 1 trillion. It is written 1,000,000,000,000.

  In trillions, you can count up to 999 trillions.

  You can write a 15-place numeral, such as the one shown below:

TRILLIONS			BILLIONS			MILLIONS			THOUSANDS			ONES		
100'S	10'S	1'S	100'S	10'S	1'S	100'S	10'S	1'S	100'S	10'S	1'S	100'S	10'S	1'S
3	8	7	4	9	6	2	7	1	5	6	9	3	2	8

= 387,496,271,569,328

- In any numeral, from the right to left:
- a. The first 3 digits stand for ones.

  They are called the ones period.

  564,489,207,138,607

- b. The second 3 digits stand for thousands.

  They are called the thousands period.
- c. The third 3 digits stand for millions.

  They are called the millions period.
- d. The fourth 3 digits stand for billions.

  They are called the billions period.
- e. The fifth 3 digits stand for trillions.

  They are called the trillions period.

- Using the number periods, you can read and write any numeral:
- a. 5,000,007 is read "five million seven."
- b. 185,000,097 is read, "one hundred eighty-five million ninety-seven."
- c. 28,785,439,370 is read, "twenty-eight billion seven hundred eighty-five million four hundred thirty-nine thousand three hundred seventy."
- d. Three million seven hundred eighty thousand five hundred ninety is written 3,780,509.
- e. Seventeen billion eight million ninety thousand twenty-four is written 17,008,090,024.

APPLICATIONS

1. In the numeral to the right: | 270,084,650,100,903
    a. What does 6 represent?   6 H's of millions
    b. What does 4 represent?   4 billions
    c. What does 7 represent?   7 T's of trillions
    d. What does 1 represent?   1 H of thousands
    e. What does 8 represent?   8 T's of billions
    f. What does 2 represent?   2 H's of trillions

2. a. Write the number which is 275 thousand
        more than 5 million.   5,275,000
    b. Write the number which is 3 hundred
        more than 7 million.   7,000,300
    c. Write the number which is 6 million
        more than 8 billion.   8,006,000,000
    d. Write the number which is 29 more
        than 17 million.   17,000,029
    e. Write the number which is 127 more
        than 4 trillion.   4,000,000,000,127

3. a. Write the number which is read
        "nine million seventeen thousand."   9,017,000
    b. Write the number which is read,
        "six billion nine thousand."   6,000,009,000
    c. Write the number which is read,
        "Four trillion twenty six."   4,000,000,000,026
    d. Write the number which is read,
        "Ninety trillion, three billion."   90,003,000,000,000

4. a. How many thousands are in 5 millions?   5,000
    b. How many millions are in 8 billions?   8,000
    c. How many billions are in 7 trillions?   7,000
    d. How many thousands are in 1 billion?   1,000,000
    e. How many millions are in 1 trillion?   1,000,000

5. a. How many millions are in 6,000 thousands?   6
    b. How many billions are in 9,000 millions?   9
    c. How many trillions are in 7,000 billions?   7

Level 12

C

EXERCISES

In adding, subtracting, multiplying, and dividing large numbers, you follow the same procedures you have followed before. You only have to be careful in placing the digits in their appropriate places.

1. Add:

a.	924,395,864 271,480,698 721,364,872 + 694,279,488 2,611,520,922	b.	9,736,207 1,600,914 2,787,227 + 5,509,352 19,633,700	c.	3,518,398,724 9,614,804,207 8,907,008,493 + 14,258,679,999 36,298,891,423

2. Subtract:

a.	23,764,271 - 9,864,936 13,899,335	b.	25,300,948 - 9,484,672 15,816,276	c.	14,000,000 - 3,708,694 10,291,306
d.	314,268,007 - 98,279,948 215,988,059	e.	279,416,000 - 68,172,904 211,243,096	f.	310,000,000 - 71,604,702 238,395,298

3. Multiply:

a.	9,429,376 x 8 75,435,008	b.	34,279,588 x 5 171,397,940	c.	2,397,648,789 x 8 19,181,190,312
d.	9,748 x 269 87732 58488 19496 2,622,212	e.	17,978 x 3,006 107868 53934 54,041,868	f.	13,908 x 4,605 69540 83448 55632 64,046,340

4. Divide:

a.	07,789,569 5) 38,947,845	b.	082,663,045 9) 743,967,405	c.	0,391,352,656 7) 2,739,468,592
d.	197,617,050 4) 790,468,200	e.	061,209,255 8) 489,674,040	f.	120,018,051 6) 720,108,306

1. From 1970 to 1980, the population of the United States of America increased from 203,235,000 to 226,546,000.
   How much was the increase?

   $$\begin{array}{r} 226,546,000 \\ -\ 203,235,000 \\ \hline 23,311,000 \end{array}$$

2. According to the 1980 census, the three most popular states were:

   California 23,667,900
   New York 17,558,100
   Texas 14,229,200

   a. How many more people lived in California than in New York?   6,109,800

   b. How many fewer people lived Texas than in New York?   3,328,900

3. Long Island (New York) is composed of two counties: Nassau and Suffolk. The table to the right gives the population of the two counties in 1970 and 1980.

	1970	1980
Nassau	1,428,838	1,321,600
Suffolk	1,127,030	1,284,200

   a. In 1970, how many people lived on Long Island?   2,555,868

   b. In 1980, how many people lived on Long Island?   2,605,800

   c. What was the increase from 1970 to 1980?   49,932

4. The difference between two numbers is 29,384,600.

a. If the smaller number is 15,183,968, what is the other number?	b. If the larger number is 40,000,200, what is the other number?
$\begin{array}{r} 29,384,600 \\ +\ 15,183,968 \\ \hline 44,568,568 \end{array}$	$\begin{array}{r} 40,000,200 \\ -\ 29,384,600 \\ \hline 10,615,600 \end{array}$

5. A is 3,967,426 less than B.

a. If A is 2,784,271, what number is B? $\begin{array}{r} 3,967,426 \\ +\ 2,784,271 \\ \hline 6,751,697 \end{array}$	b. If B is 5,405,207, what number is A? $\begin{array}{r} 5,405,207 \\ -\ 3,967,426 \\ \hline 1,437,781 \end{array}$

6. M is 5 times N.

a. If N is 8,648,435, what number is M? $\begin{array}{r} 8,648,435 \\ \times\quad\ \ 5 \\ \hline 43,242,175 \end{array}$	b. If M is 8,648,435. what number is N? $\begin{array}{r} 1,729,687 \\ \hline 5)\ 8,648,435 \end{array}$

UNIT C TEST

1. a. Use the digits 5, 3, 2, 9, 0, 8.
      to form the largest number you can.   985,320
   b. Use the digits 5, 3, 2, 9, 0, 8
      to form the smallest number you can.   023,589

2. a. In the numeral 321,425 what does 1 stand for?   1 thousand
   b. In the numeral 321,425 what does 3 stand for?   3 H's of Th's

3. a. How many T's of Th's are in 3H's of Th's ?   30
   b. How many T's of Th's are in 60 Th's?   6
   c. How would you group 94 Th's?   9 T's of Th and 4 Th's

4. Add:

a.	234,102	b.	136,129	c.	123,766	d.	251,938
	101,341		213,937		98,838		51,791
	42,013		89,853		76,199		272,787
	+ 321,321		67,086		120,484		103,470
	698,777		+ 109,795		+ 53,252		+ 60,014
			616,800		472,539		740,000

5. Subtract:

a.	987,645	b.	837,612	c.	380,726	d.	700,000
	- 264,231		- 18,729		- 99,213		- 271,842
	723,414		818,883		281,513		428,158

6. A is a number. You subtracted
   85,729 and then added 98,401.
   The answer was 300,000.   a. 300,000 - 98,401 = 201,599
   What was the number?   b. 201,599 + 85,729 = 287,328

7. Subtract the sum of 398,271 and   a. 398,271 + 179,306 = 577,577
   179,306 from 800,000.   b. 800,000 - 577,577 = 222,423

8. N - 379,668 = 209,467
   What number is N?   N = 209,467 + 379,668 = 589,135

9. Multiply:
   a. 2 x 243,412 = __486,824__
   b. 6 x 38,432 = __230,592__
   c. 3 x 68,273 = __204,819__
   d. 8 x 86,325 = __690,600__

10. Multiply:
    a. 100 x 100 = __10,000__
    b. 100 x 1,000 = __100,000__
    c. 50 x 400 = __20,000__
    d. 700 x 60 = __42,000__
    e. 600 x 600 = __360,000__
    f. 80 x 3,000 = __240,000__

11. Multiply:
    a. 90 x 378 = __34,020__
    b. 3000 x 29 = __87,000__
    c. 316 x 200 = __63,200__
    d. 314 x 500 = __157,000__
    e. 78 x 5000 = __390,000__
    f. 1230 x 400 = __492,000__

12. Multiply:

a.	b.	c.
972 x 48 7776 3888 46656	804 x 25 4020 1608 20100	950 x 38 7600 2850 36100

d.	e.	f.
675 x 328 5400 1350 2025 221400	256 x 490 2304 1024 125440	723 x 105 3615 72300 75915

13. Divide:

a.	b.	c.
$\underline{421,342}$ 2) 842,684	$\underline{210,031}$ 3) 630,093	$\underline{151,967}$ 5) 759,835

d.	e.	f.
$\underline{032,298}$ 8) 258,384	$\underline{130,893}$ 6) 785,358	$\underline{090,031}$ 4) 360,124

14. Divide:

a.	b.	c.
00461 29) 13369 116 176 174 29 29	00105 549) 57645 549 2745 2745	00390 235) 91650 705 2115 2115

15. On weekdays a newspaper sells
93,728 copies daily. On Sunday
it sells 34,625 copies more.
How many copies are sold in one week?

a. 6 x 93,728 = 562,368
b. 93,728 + 34,625 = 128,353
c. 562,368 + 128,353 = 690,721

16. a. You have 39,168 items. You want to
divide them into sets, 128 items each.
What is the result?   306 sets are made.
b. You have 39,168 items. You want to
divide them equally into 128 sets.
What is the result?   306 items in each set.

$$\begin{array}{r} 00306 \\ 128 \overline{)39168} \\ 384 \\ \hline 768 \\ 768 \end{array}$$

17. A builder spent $600,000 on 6 identical
houses. He paid $147,750 for the land
and the rest was spent on construction.
How much was spent on the construction
of each house?

a. $600,000 - $147,750 = $452,250
b. $452,250 ÷ 6 = $75,375

18. The sum of two numbers is 235,000.
One of the numbers is 95,658.
What is the other number?

235,000 - 95,658 = 139,342

19. 7 x a number is 468,314.
What is the number?

468,314 ÷ 7 = 66,902

20. N = 325 x 218
M = N - 25000
What number is M?

a. N = 70,850
b. M = 70,850 - 25,000 = 45,850

21. a. What is a million?   1,000 thousands
b. What is a billion?   1,000 millions
c. What is a trillion?   1,000 billions

22. The letters to the right stand for digits in a numeral.   YMH,CAD,BXM,GNF,TVS
a. What does N stand for?   tens of thousands
b. What does X stand for?   tens of millions
c. What does Y stand for?   hundreds of trillions

23. Write the numeral which is read:
    a. Seven million six thousand — 7,006,000
    b. Twenty-eight billion three million — 28,003,000,000
    c. Nine billion thirty-five — 9,000,000,035
    d. Eight billion six million four — 8,006,000,004

24. a. Write the number which is 35 million more than 7 billion. — 7,035,000,000
    b. Write the number which is 85 more than 6 million. — 6,000,085
    c. Write the number which is 80 thousand more than 26 million. — 26,080,000

25. Add:

a.	b.	c.
379,268,494	7,480,618	360,789,248
39,607,320	2,976,314	438,216,843
+ 48,268,481	+ 4,097,026	+ 273,625,909
467,144,295	14,553,958	1,072,632,000

26. Subtract:

a.	b.	c.
39,648,271	87,263,000	90,000,000
- 9,423,784	- 48,372,976	- 48,304,206
30,224,487	38,890,024	41,695,794

27. Multiply:

a.	b.	c.
15,706	3,504	12,107
x 2,009	x 924	x 3,201
141,354	14,016	12,107
31,412,000	70,080	2,421,400
31,553,354	3,153,600	36,321,000
	3,237,696	38,754,507

28. Divide:

a.	b.	c.
04,234,375	11,682,168	027,090,306
8) 33,875,000	6) 70,093,008	5) 135,451,530

29. The population of a state changed from 2,678,287 to 3,107,569. What was the change?

$$3,107,569 - 2,678,287 = 429,282$$
An increase of 429,282 people

30. What number do you multiply by 8 for the product to be 300,832,416?

$$300,832,416 \div 8 = 37,604,052$$

Level 12

31. Using only the digits to the right: 2, 5, 9, 4, 3, 1, 0

    a. What is the largest number you can write?   _9,543,210_

    b. What is the smallest number you can write?   _123,459_

    c. What is the sum of the the two numbers?   _9,666,669_

    d. What is the difference between the two numbers?   _9,419,751_

32. A, B, and C are three numbers. A is 9,673,109 and B is 2,683,298. A + B + C is
15,000,000. What number is C?

                                          _2,643,593_

$C = 15,000,000 - (A + B)$
$= 15,000,000 - (9,673,109 + 2,683,298)$
$= 15,000,000 - 12,356,407$

33. The sum of two numbers 90,000. One number is 10,000 greater than the other?

    a. What is the smaller number?   _40,000_

$\frac{1}{2} \times (90,000 - 10,000)$
$\frac{1}{2} \times 80,000$

    b. What is the larger number?   _50,000_
40,000 + 10,000